Russel Wright's

MENU COOKBOOK

A guide to easier entertaining

Russel Wright's

MENU COOKBOOK

A guide to easier entertaining

Ann Wright and Mindy Heiferling

Foreword by Martha Stewart

Photographs by Beatriz Da Costa and James Demarest

Gibbs Smith, Publisher
Salt Lake City

First Edition
08 07 06 05 04 03   5 4 3 2 1

Text © 2003 by Ann Wright and Mindy Heiferling
Photographs © 2003 by Beatriz Da Costa and James Demarest

Published by
Gibbs Smith, Publisher
P.O. Box 667
Layton, Utah 84041

Orders: 1.800.748.5439
www.gibbs-smith.com

Edited by Suzanne Gibbs Taylor
Designed and produced by Bryan Burkhart / MODERNHOUSE
Printed and bound in Hong Kong

Library of Congress Cataloging-in-Publication Data

Wright, Ann.
       Russel Wright's menu cookbook : a guide to easier entertaining /
       Ann Wright and Mindy Heiferling.– 1st ed.
              p. cm. Includes index.
       ISBN 1-58685-281-7
1. Entertaining. 2. Cookery. 3. Menus. I. Heiferling, Mindy.
       II. Wright, Russel, 1904-1976. III. Title.

TX731 .W727 2003
642'.4–dc21
                              2002153922

To Margaret Spader, my father's best friend in the kitchen and the inspiration behind our family's *Menu Cookbook*. Margaret taught us both how to cook and organize ourselves in the kitchen. Without her friendship and advice, this book would not exist.

   —Ann

To my aunt Lily Liss, for her love for me and her passion for midcentury Modern.

   —Mindy

ACKNOWLEDGEMENTS

We both wish to thank—Our editor, Suzanne Taylor, whose patience and good nature is truly an inspiration; Gibbs Smith and his team, for seeing the potential and making it happen; Paul Gebhart, our visionary and project mentor; Peter Brown, for his wonderful sense of Russel Wright and design, and the expert team from Oneida, including our stylist, Melinda Cross; Bryan Burkhart, for designing the book we envisioned; Dennis Mykytyn, for lending us some of his treasured collection to photograph and for his invaluable support of the Russel Wright Studios; the staff at Manitoga, the Russel Wright Design Center, for their great generosity in allowing us to photograph where the *Menu Cookbook* was originally planned and primarily used; Bill Straus, who saved the day with his Russel Wright aluminum collection; and to Mood Indigo in New York City, for loaning us photography props.

Mindy wishes to thank—

My friends and family, near and far, who are always there for me; and Annie Wright, for her friendship and for providing me with the great opportunity to combine my love of food and design.

To contact and learn more about Manitoga:

www.russelwrightcenter.org
Email: info@russelwrightcenter.org
Phone: 845.424.3812

Additional photo credits:
Pages 10, 60-61, 132 top and bottom, and 134—From the collection of Ann Wright.
Page 8-9—Courtesy of Adam Anik.
Page 136, bottom—Courtesy of Farrell Grehan.

Contents

Foreword

In 2001, the Cooper-Hewitt Museum staged an important retrospective of the designs and philosophy of living of Mary and Russel Wright. The exhibit was an eye-opener for me, for despite the fact that I had collected an assortment of Russel Wright tableware—most notably my favorite dinnerware, granite-gray American modern—I was uninformed about the couple's very real devotion to teaching and instructing masses of mid-twentieth-century homemakers the fine points of beautiful utilitarian practical living.

It was the Wrights' goal to create and endorse an informal, modern, functional, and comfortable lifestyle that was casual without being sloppy, and that was based on fine design and carefully crafted objects, fashioned from functional materials, that would be long-lived and contemporary.

From the 1930s to the late '60s, the Wrights were the leading proponents of what is now known as all-American modernism, and in 1950 they published *Guide to Easier Living*. I had not read that book until after the exhibit and it was so peculiar when I finally did, for the Wrights wrote and thought and taught very much as I do today. Just like them, I, and everyone I work with, am dedicated to bringing the best ideas, the best recipes, the best design, and the best sensibilities and "newness" to everyday living, without sacrificing history, traditions, beauty, and family.

Annie Wright, Russel Wright's daughter, and Mindy Heiferling should be proud of their classic and well-produced rendition of Wright's recipes and tips for casual, lovely, and delicious food that is wonderfully presented. The recipes are mouthwatering yet simple, the table settings fine yet casual, and the information as timely today as when it was originally compiled more than 50 years ago.

Martha Stewart

Introduction

Growing up in New York in the 1950s as the daughter of two prominent and successful designers, Russel and Mary Wright, I was truly a child of midcentury Modern. My parents pioneered products for the home—furniture, flatware, glassware, rugs, lamps, pottery, table linens, and jukeboxes—that have become highly collectible design icons. Mass-produced and at affordable prices, their designs were functional, practical, and beautiful, geared toward the, more informal post–World-War II American lifestyle. (Their American Modern was the best-selling line of dinnerware in U.S. history, with people lining up outside department stores when new shipments arrived.) They believed in the value of good American design and ingenuity, and eschewed the fussy Euro-centric and stodgy American Traditional styles that were then popular. They also believed in reducing the amount of time people had become accustomed to spending on household chores, and in 1950 wrote *The Guide to Easier Living*, which became an instant success.

After my mother died in 1952 when I was two years old, my father was faced with organizing our lives in a manner that permitted him to work and be a single parent at the same time. In those early days we were graced with a wonderful nanny named Mamie Mitchell. She did just about everything and anything to help us, but cooking was not her greatest strength. Mamie's repertoire consisted of two complete menus: spaghetti, meatballs, salad, and chocolate pudding and I believe that meatloaf and mashed potatoes with varying accompaniments was the other. We would readily consume one of these menus one night and alternate with the other the following night. As anyone can imagine, this became quite tiresome very quickly. As a solution, my father conceived *Russel Wright's Menu Cookbook*.

This cookbook left no room for error in preparation, presentation, or coordination. Bound in a loose-leaf notebook, it was a compilation of roughly 100 recipes with pencil notations everywhere. The instructions were explicit and the message clear: Allow the food to speak for itself; do not use overly decorated plates or ostentatious table settings that distract from the food; and make mealtime preparation as easy as possible by doing many things ahead of time or by purchasing high-quality ready-made products. Hence, anyone should be able to shop, cook, and set the table with pleasing results and a minimum of time and labor. For example, a lamb curry dinner was expected to be served on chutney-brown American Modern dinnerware to best enhance the color combinations, textures, and general presentation. Interwoven into our dinnerware were serving accessories from my father's travels in Southeast Asia and Africa. The idea was to entertain with ease, whether it was with new guests or with your own family. Our household ran smoothly around mealtimes, and to this day I stand in awe of the ease with which this cookbook allowed us to create delicious meals served on our various sets of Russel Wright dinnerware.

Russel's continued success as one of this country's most celebrated and innovative industrial designers made him a leader and authority on the American lifestyle. It has been said that he invented lifestyle marketing, a concept now commonly used in the marketplace. His vision, along with the unexpected role of single parent, put him in a position to practice his theories on easier living, entertaining, and preparing everyday meals in an organized, stylish, and creative manner. Russel led the American public into the new era of ease and convenience necessary in a world of two-income or single-parent households where time management was crucial.

The following menus are many of Russel's and my favorites. They were acquired at dinner parties or shared with us by other food enthusiasts. Margaret Spader, George Lang, Tom Margittai, and Amy Vanderbilt were among the contributors. These menus were originally geared toward our neighborhood in midtown Manhattan. As I grew older, my father would send

me to our corner drugstore on 48th and Third Avenue for a pint of Louis Sherry's peach ice cream or even farther afield to Horn & Hardart for lemon meringue pie. (Oh, how I loved putting those nickels and dimes in the slots and watching the food rotate.) Alas, these landmarks are gone, but new neighborhood bakeries and specialty food stores have sprung up, not just in my old New York neighborhood, but everywhere. Supermarkets now have frozen pie dough and phyllo, imported olive oils, artisan breads, cheeses, and a huge selection of what was once exotic produce. Our lives today are busier and more complicated than ever. Make your life easier: use these products in your meal planning as we did in ours.

My fascination with food and my early indoctrination into mealtime preparation led me to pursue a gratifying career in the food world, first as a restaurant chef, and more recently as a caterer. It was through catering that I met and became friends with Mindy Heiferling, who became my collaborator on this first published version of *Russel Wright's Menu Cookbook*. After paging through the original cookbook and seeing my father's meticulous planning and specific instructions for what food to put on what platter, Mindy's first comment was, "Annie, you were born to be a caterer!" We sorted through the menus and recipes and chose those we thought were the best and most representative of how and what my father and I ate in those days, yet were also appealing to modern tastes and suited to modern lifestyles.

As a working mother, I still make use of my treasured family menus, and for this I can only thank my parents and their friends who contributed to our daily rituals surrounding *Russel Wright's Menu Cookbook*.

Ann Wright

MIDSUMMER AMERICANA COOKOUT

ADVANCE PREPARATION NOTES

2 DAYS BEFORE THE COOKOUT

Make Flank Steak Marinade. Soak beans.

1 DAY BEFORE THE COOKOUT

Marinate flank steak. Mix ingredients for Cliff House Sauce; put in a small covered container and refrigerate.

Make Chopped Coleslaw; refrigerate, covered, in a serving bowl.

Make Baked Beans, or boil beans and set up in a baking dish with remaining ingredients and bake tomorrow.

DAY OF THE COOKOUT

Set up a tray with everything you need to barbecue: tongs, mitts, paper towels, serving platters for steak (and oysters if you plan to grill instead of bake them), salt and pepper in plastic containers, a meat thermometer, a spray bottle with water, and a damp rag for your hands.

4 HOURS BEFORE GUESTS ARRIVE

Slice watermelon in wedges and put on serving platter in refrigerator.

1 HOUR BEFORE GUESTS ARRIVE

Prepare ingredients for Baked Oysters, put in a baking dish, and refrigerate until ready to bake.

Assemble Green Corn Pudding, put in baking dish, and refrigerate until ready to bake.

Remove meat from refrigerator 1 hour before grilling.

Reheat baked beans.

Cut peaches shortly before serving dessert.

One of my fondest childhood memories is of shucking bushels of corn at the home of Gladys Denny Schultz, our Garrison, New York, neighbor. Gladys, a gifted writer and cook, was one of Russel's best friends, who spent many evenings at Dragon Rock, as we did at her house. Originally from Iowa, Gladys would buy bushels and bushels of corn every July and August and have her grandchildren and me shuck them and cut the kernels off of the cob. She would then freeze them for use in the Green Corn Pudding recipe. It was a homey and spirited time, often spurred on with Gladys's homemade ice cream. The recipe is truly a delicious corn pudding, memorable for any occasion.

MENU (serves 6)

Baked or Grilled Oysters

Marinated Flank Steak with Cliff House Sauce

Baked Beans

Chopped Coleslaw

Green Corn Pudding

Vanilla Ice Cream with Peaches and Berries

Watermelon Slices

Tip for Grilled Oysters

Buy fresh oysters in the shell, scrub well with a brush under cold running water, and cook on the grill while the flank steak rests. Oysters are done when the shells are fully open. Serve on a platter lined with seaweed (available, usually for free, from the fish market) or rock salt, accompanied by a bowl of melted butter with a little lemon juice and Tabasco added.

Baked Oysters

3 tablespoons finely chopped thick-cut bacon

1 quart fresh shucked oysters, drained and picked through for pieces of shell

1 tablespoon fresh-squeezed lemon juice, plus additional to finish

Kosher salt and freshly ground pepper to taste

1 tablespoon finely chopped scallion (white and light green parts only)

1 tablespoon finely chopped flat-leaf parsley

1 medium garlic clove, mashed or grated to a fine purée

Dry bread crumbs

1 tablespoon unsalted butter

Fruity olive oil for drizzling

1. Cut the bacon into small pieces and line a buttered shallow casserole (such as a 10-inch oval gratin dish) with 1/3 of it.

2. Toss the oysters with the lemon juice, salt and pepper, scallion, parsley, and garlic; spread half of the mixture over the bacon in the casserole in an even layer. Add half the remaining bacon and repeat with the rest of the oysters and bacon. Sprinkle with breadcrumbs and dot with butter.

3. Bake in a preheated 350-degree oven until the mixture is bubbling at the edges, about 15 minutes. Just before serving, top with a squirt of lemon juice and a generous drizzle of olive oil.

Marinated Flank Steak with Cliff House Sauce

3 pounds flank steak

Marinade

6 tablespoons Dijon mustard

6 tablespoons soy sauce

1-1/2 teaspoons Worcestershire sauce

1 tablespoon red wine vinegar

1 tablespoon fruity olive oil

3/4 teaspoon coarsely ground black pepper

2 teaspoons coarsely chopped fresh rosemary

3 large garlic cloves, peeled and sliced

Kosher salt to taste

Cliff House Sauce

1 garlic clove, minced to a paste with kosher salt

4 teaspoons Worcestershire sauce

4 tablespoons unsalted butter

1 teaspoon dry mustard

Freshly ground black pepper to taste

1. To marinate the steak, whisk the mustard, soy sauce, Worcestershire, and vinegar together until smooth. Whisk in the olive oil, then add the pepper, rosemary, and garlic. Put the steak in a nonreactive container, turn to coat with the marinade, cover, and refrigerate overnight.

2. Wipe most of the marinade off with a paper towel and salt the meat.

3. Prepare a gas or charcoal fire (or heat a couple of heavy skillets filmed with oil). When the coals are covered with white ash, put the meat on the grill; cook about 6 minutes per side for medium-rare (an instant-read thermometer inserted sideways through the center of the meat should read 120 degrees). Do not cook past medium-rare; flank steak will toughen and dry up if you do.

4. Let the meat rest, loosely covered with foil, for 10 minutes.

5. Make the sauce while the meat rests. Combine the sauce ingredients in a small saucepan (you can do this on the grill or the stovetop) over medium heat until bubbling.

6. Slice the meat against the grain and serve with Cliff House Sauce.

Grilling Tip

When grilling or searing this or any other food, give it time to develop a crust on one side before turning it. If it seems to be sticking to the grill when you try to turn it, leave it alone for a couple of minutes; when it has developed a good crust, it will turn easily.

Baked Beans

1/2 pound navy (pea) beans, rinsed and soaked overnight in water

2 to 3 ounces salt pork

3 tablespoons dark brown sugar

3 tablespoons ketchup

3 tablespoons molasses

1 teaspoon cider vinegar

1/2 teaspoon Dijon mustard

1-1/2 teaspoons dry mustard

1/16 teaspoon ground ginger

1/4 of a medium onion, peeled, root end trimmed but left attached

Kosher salt and freshly ground black pepper to taste

1. Drain the beans and put in a pot with water to cover by several inches. Bring to a simmer and cook, covered, until tender, about 45 minutes to 1 hour, depending on the age of the beans. Add salt to taste when the beans are almost done. Save the cooking liquid.

2. Cut the salt pork into 1/4-inch dice and cook in a pot of boiling water for 3 minutes.

3. In a casserole or bean pot, combine the beans with the remaining ingredients and enough of the bean liquid to come just to the level of the beans. Bring to a simmer.

4. Bake, covered, at 300 degrees for 1 hour; remove the lid and cook until the sauce thickens slightly and gets darker, about 20 minutes. Remove the onion before serving.

Sticky Liquid Tip

Molasses, honey, corn syrup, or any sticky liquid will pour easily from the measuring cup if you spray the cup with vegetable oil first.

Chopped Coleslaw

4 tablespoons cider vinegar

3 tablespoons Dijon mustard

4 teaspoons honey

Kosher salt and freshly ground
black pepper to taste

1/2 cup mayonnaise

1/4 cup sour cream

1/2 teaspoon celery seed

1 teaspoon minced jalapeño pepper

1/2 of a small savoy or green
cabbage, cored (about 3/4 pound)

1 medium carrot, peeled and trimmed

1/3 cup diced red or yellow pepper

4 teaspoons finely chopped scallion,
white and light green parts only

1. In a bowl, whisk together the vinegar, mustard, honey, salt, and pepper. Whisk in the mayonnaise, sour cream, celery seed, and jalapeño until smooth.

2. Cut the cabbage into chunks about 2 inches around and put in the work bowl of a food processor. Pulse about 10 times, until the cabbage is in 1/4-inch pieces. Add to the bowl with the dressing.

3. Cut the carrot into chunks and pulse in the food processor until the pieces are the same size as the cabbage. Add to the bowl with the cabbage and dressing.

4. Add the red pepper and scallion to the bowl; mix until blended. Chill for an hour or more before serving.

Green Corn Pudding

"Green" simply means fresh corn, and the time to make this dish is in summer with farm-fresh corn. This is an unusually silky and delicate-tasting pudding, so pure in flavor that it really needs nothing else to accent it. However, if you'd like to serve this as a more substantial lunch dish (accompanied by a green salad, perhaps), add Cheddar, Gruyere, Muenster, or Parmesan cheese or some chopped, roasted poblano chilies.

5 ears of corn

1/2 cup half-and-half

2 large eggs, beaten

2 tablespoons unsalted butter, melted

1 tablespoon flour

1/4 teaspoon sugar

3/4 teaspoon kosher salt

Freshly ground black pepper to taste

Chopped chives or basil for garnish

1. Husk the corn, remove the silk, and, with the large-hole side of a box grater, grate the kernels into a bowl. With the dull side of a knife and holding the corn over the bowl, scrape the cob well to extract the milky liquid that remains.

2. Add the remaining ingredients except for the herbs, whisk gently to blend, and transfer to a buttered shallow baking dish, about 1-1/2 inches high and 9 to 10 inches across (choose an attractive one that the pudding can also be served in).

3. Bake in a preheated 350-degree oven until a toothpick inserted in the center comes out clean, 25 to 30 minutes. Let rest for 5 minutes before cutting. Garnish with chives or basil if desired.

COLD SALAD BUFFET FOR SUMMER

ADVANCE PREPARATION NOTES

3 DAYS BEFORE THE BUFFET

Prepare and refrigerate all dressings.

2 DAYS BEFORE THE BUFFET

Clean, dry, and refrigerate greens.

Roast or poach chicken; dice, cover, and refrigerate.

Pit cherries for Cherry Pudding.

1 DAY BEFORE THE BUFFET

Prepare grapefruit, celery, cucumber, pepper for the Chicken Salad; cover and refrigerate.

Prepare bell pepper, scallion, and green beans for the Moss Green Salad; cover and refrigerate.

Pit cherries for Cherry Pudding if not done earlier.

DAY OF THE BUFFET

If serving Cherry Pudding at room temperature, bake it a few hours before guests arrive.

If serving Cherry Pudding warm, bake it right before the party begins.

In our family, summers were most often busy, hot and humid, and generally spent outdoors. We had a white wooden picnic table and benches set up close to a rock waterfall, which gave us a sense of coolness even in hundred-degree weather. This chicken salad, with its nontraditional addition of grapefruit, is also refreshing and cool.

Russel was always precise in his directions with coordinating table settings. For this particular menu, we used white snow-glass plates, further promoting a cool, icy feeling through color and texture. And as busy as many of us are, this menu can be served at lunch or dinner and prepared well in advance. It is especially nice in the summertime to serve all the salads in bowls or plates chilled in the fridge or by filling the bowls with ice for awhile, and then wiping them dry.

MENU (serves 8)

Gourmet Chicken Salad

Moss Green Salad with Sour Cream Dressing

Multicolored Tomatoes and Corn with Creamy Cider Vinaigrette

Assorted Breads and Rolls

Cherry Pudding

Gourmet Chicken Salad

1 grapefruit

2 cups diced cooked chicken

1/2 cup finely chopped celery

1/2 cup thinly sliced red or yellow
  bell pepper

1/4 cup diced cucumber

1/2 cup vinaigrette (recipe below)

Kosher salt and freshly ground pepper
  to taste

1/2 cup mayonnaise

1 teaspoon curry powder

1 teaspoon grated onion

1 teaspoon chopped flat-leaf parsley,
  plus extra for garnish

1 teaspoon chopped chives

Boston lettuce leaves, cleaned and
  chilled, to line platter

1/2 cup chopped salted peanuts

2 teaspoons drained and rinsed capers

Paprika to garnish

1. With a sharp chef's knife or bread knife, cut the bottom and top ends off the grapefruit so it can lie flat. Remove the skin and white pith by cutting down the grapefruit from top to bottom, working your way around, trying to keep the shape of the fruit round as you go. Holding the fruit in your hand, cut out the sections by inserting the knife next to the side of each membrane, then cutting down. Set aside.

2. Combine the chicken, celery, bell pepper, and cucumber in a bowl with the vinaigrette. Season with salt and pepper; mix well, then cover and refrigerate for 2 to 3 hours.

3. Mix the mayonnaise with the curry powder, grated onion, 1 teaspoon of chopped parsley, and chives. Stir into the chicken salad.

4. Line a platter with lettuce, spoon chicken salad onto the leaves, and lay the grapefruit sections on top. Sprinkle the salad with peanuts, capers, paprika, and chopped parsley.

Vinaigrette

1/2 teaspoon Dijon mustard

2 tablespoons white wine
  vinegar

6 tablespoons olive oil

Kosher salt and pepper to taste

1/2 cup mayonnaise

Whisk all ingredients together in a bowl.

Moss Green Salad with Sour Cream Dressing

Russel made this salad in the days before baby spinach and haricots vert were available in supermarkets. I love baby spinach for its taste and convenience—it's often sold already cleaned. Feel free to substitute baby spinach and haricots for the spinach and string beans when you make this. It's a good idea to make the dressing before the salad and let it sit, covered and chilled, to let the flavors develop.

Dressing

1 cup sour cream

2 scallions, ends trimmed, rinsed, and cut into large pieces

2 tablespoons mayonnaise

2 to 3 tablespoons freshly squeezed lemon juice

1/2 cup crumbled Bleu cheese

Kosher salt and freshly ground black pepper to taste

Salad

1 pound spinach, preferably baby or flat-leaf

1 bunch watercress

1/2 head escarole

2 green bell peppers

1/2 cup thinly sliced scallion greens or chives

1/2 pound green beans or haricots vert

For dressing

Combine the ingredients in a blender or food processor and blend until smooth.

For salad

1. Wash spinach, trim thick stems from watercress, and wash escarole. Dry well and chill. Cut off the top and a bit of the bottom from the green peppers and slice thin, lengthwise. Combine with scallions. Chill.

2. Trim stem ends from beans and cook in a pot of rapidly boiling salted water until crisp and tender, about 2 minutes. Transfer to a colander and rinse under cold water. Dry well. Chill.

3. To serve, combine all the salad ingredients in a bowl, season with salt and pepper, then pour the dressing over the salad. Toss to coat the vegetables with the dressing.

Multicolored Tomatoes and Corn with Creamy Cider Vinaigrette

3 tablespoons cider vinegar

3 tablespoons Dijon mustard

1 tablespoon sugar

1/2 cup mayonnaise

1 tablespoon chopped tarragon or basil

Kosher salt and freshly ground
black pepper to taste

2 pounds ripe tomatoes in various colors,
shapes, and sizes, cut into wedges

3 cups (about 6 ears) fresh corn
kernels, cooked

6 slices bacon, cooked until crisp and
crumbled (optional)

Tarragon sprigs or basil leaves for
garnish

1. Whisk together the vinegar, mustard, sugar, and mayonnaise. Stir in the tarragon or basil; season to taste with salt and pepper. Combine with tomatoes and corn; taste again for seasonings.

2. When ready to serve (don't wait too long or the tomatoes will make the salad too watery), transfer to a bowl or platter, and top with bacon and herbs if desired.

Cherry Pudding

Similar to a cobbler, this dish is wonderful when served hot or warm.

2 cups sifted flour

2 teaspoons baking powder

1-1/3 cups sugar

Pinch of kosher salt

2/3 cup milk

2 tablespoons melted unsalted butter

2-1/2 cups pitted and drained red
cherries, fresh, canned, or frozen,
juice reserved

2 tablespoons unsalted butter

2-2/3 cups hot water or cherry juice
and water

Whipped cream or ice cream (optional)

1. Preheat oven to 375 degrees.

2. Sift flour, baking powder, half the sugar, and salt together in a bowl. Add milk and melted butter; stir until smooth. Spread evenly in an 8-1/2 x 3-1/2-inch round baking dish; arrange the cherries on top. Combine the hot liquid with the remaining sugar and butter; bring to a boil. Pour over the cherries and immediately put into the oven. Bake until cherries rise to the surface and pudding has puffed up and absorbed a good portion of the cherry liquid, about 60 minutes.

3. Serve warm with whipped cream or ice cream if desired.

DINNER FOR A SUMMER NIGHT

ADVANCE PREPARATION NOTES

3 DAYS BEFORE THE DINNER

Roast tomatoes and red peppers. Peel and refrigerate. (This step can also be done ahead of time and the ingredients frozen.)

2 DAYS BEFORE THE DINNER

Prepare remainder of soup and chill.

Squeeze limes or lemons and grate the rinds. Combine the juice and grated rinds; refrigerate. (A zester is a very handy tool for grating the rind and can be purchased at most cooking supply stores.)

Prepare Curry Dressing for Crab Ravigote.

1 DAY BEFORE THE DINNER

Prepare remainder of Lime or Lemon Soufflé; refrigerate.

DAY OF THE DINNER

Prepare Crab Ravigote.

Crabmeat of good quality needs very little added to it. This recipe enhances its flavor without disguising it. The soup can use red, orange, or yellow tomatoes and peppers to vary its visual appeal. Roasting peppers and tomatoes together creates a delicious combination reminiscent of a sun-dried tomato.

MENU (serves 6)

Elizabeth Winter's Chilled Tomato Soup with Yogurt Garnish

Crabmeat Ravigote in Avocado Shells with Curry Dressing

Store-bought Pappadums

Lemon or Lime Soufflé

Elizabeth Winter's Chilled Tomato Soup with Yogurt Garnish

1 medium onion, finely diced

1 tablespoon olive oil

2-1/2 pounds tomatoes
(about 8 medium or 6 large)

2 large sweet red peppers

2/3 cup fresh orange juice (2 oranges)

14-1/2 ounces fresh or canned
chicken stock

1 tablespoon balsamic vinegar

Kosher salt and pepper to taste

Chopped fresh herbs for garnish

Yogurt for garnish

1. Sauté onion in olive oil until soft and translucent, about 5 minutes or less.

2. Roast the tomatoes and red peppers on a cookie sheet in a 400-degree oven until there is a slight charring around their edges. This will take about 30 minutes but is dependent on the size of the tomatoes and the thickness of the pepper flesh.

3. Peel the roasted peppers and tomatoes.

4. Chop the onions, peppers, and tomatoes in a blender or food processor, then push them through a food mill or strainer.

5. Add orange juice, stock, vinegar, salt, and pepper; simmer for 10 minutes; refrigerate until cold. Serve with a garnish of yogurt and chopped fresh herbs.

Pepper Peeling Tip

Put the roasted peppers and tomatoes in a plastic bag in the refrigerator until cold. This makes peeling easier.

Crabmeat Ravigote in Avocado Shells with Curry Dressing

Curry Dressing

5 tablespoons mayonnaise

1 teaspoon curry powder

2 tablespoons finely chopped parsley

1/2 teaspoon red wine vinegar

1/2 teaspoon ground cumin

1/2 teaspoon finely minced garlic

1/2 teaspoon finely minced fresh ginger

1 teaspoon honey mustard

Put all ingredients in a bowl and whisk until well blended. Chill.

Crabmeat Ravigote

1 pound cooked crabmeat

1/4 cup lemon juice or tarragon vinegar

2 tablespoons finely chopped scallions

1/4 cup chopped pimiento

2 tablespoons chopped sweet pickles

1/2 cup mayonnaise

Salt and pepper to taste

Capers for garnish

3 ripe avocados, halved and skins removed (just before serving)

1. Flake crabmeat and moisten with lemon juice or tarragon vinegar. Let stand in the refrigerator for about 30 minutes.

2. Drain off the juice, pressing crabmeat lightly, and add the scallions, pimiento, sweet pickles, mayonnaise, and salt and pepper to taste.

3. Toss lightly and place on half of an avocado. Garnish with capers.

Lemon or Lime Soufflé

6 large egg yolks

1/4 cup sugar

Zest of 2 limes or lemons,
    finely grated

Juice of 3 limes or lemons

2 teaspoons gelatin dissolved in
    1/4 cup cold water

1-1/2 cups heavy cream, whipped

1 tablespoon Grand Marnier liqueur

Pinch of kosher salt

Pinch of ground ginger

1. Put egg yolks and sugar in top of double boiler over hot water. Whip until creamy and thick. Remove from heat; add lime or lemon zest and juice.

2. Return to heat; using a wire whisk, continually whip mixture until it is thick and creamy again.

3. Soak gelatin in cold water for 5 minutes. Add soaked gelatin to hot egg mixture and allow to cool. Then whip this mixture until very light.

4. Whip the cream with the Grand Marnier until stiff; fold in the salt and ginger.

5. Pour into a mold and chill thoroughly.

FALL HARVEST DINNER

ADVANCE PREPARATION NOTES

1 DAY BEFORE THE DINNER

Make apricot purée. If Apricot Whip is to be served cold, make today or early tomorrow; refrigerate.

Make Irish Stew.

Toast walnuts, clean greens, make cider vinaigrette for salad.

DAY OF THE DINNER

Separate 7 eggs; refrigerate whites, tightly covered, for Apricot Whip.

Degrease stew, reheat to serve.

This is a perfect menu for a nippy fall day when farmers' market stalls are overflowing with all sorts of root vegetables and newly harvested apples. The Irish stew is nontraditional in that the lamb is browned before the vegetables and liquid are added. This gives the finished product the richer, more complex flavor that we prefer; however, if you want to save a step or simply prefer the taste of traditional Irish stew, don't brown the meat. Marjoram is also nontraditional, but Russel always used it; it tasted great, so here it is.

MENU (serves 6)

Irish Stew with Root Vegetables

Frisée and Watercress Salad with Apples and Toasted Walnuts with Cider Vinaigrette

Apricot Whip

Irish Stew with Root Vegetables

Stews and soups are almost always better when eaten a day or two after they have been made, which makes them perfect for entertaining. Cook this stew a day or two ahead (adding the peas and parsley right before serving), and reheat it in the oven or on the stove before serving.

3 pounds boneless shoulder or leg of lamb, trimmed well and cut into 1-1/2 inch cubes

Kosher salt and freshly ground black pepper to taste

Canola oil to film bottom of pan

1 tablespoon unsalted butter

1-1/2 cups chopped leek, white and light green parts only (see "Tips")

1-1/2 tablespoons flour

3-1/2 cups (approximately) chicken stock, preferably homemade

12 small red potatoes (about 1 pound total weight), peeled and cut in half

2 small turnips (about 6 ounces total weight), peeled and cut into 1/2-inch wedges

2 carrots (about 6 ounces total weight), peeled and cut into 1/4-inch rounds

2 parsnips (about 6 ounces total weight), peeled and cut into 1/4-inch rounds

1 cup fresh or frozen pearl onions, peeled

2 teaspoons finely chopped parsley

6 tablespoons frozen petits pois (baby peas)

Bouquet Garni

1/4 teaspoon dried marjoram

3 sprigs of flat-leaf parsley

3 cloves garlic, peeled and slightly crushed

1 bay leaf

6 black peppercorns

1. Season the lamb with salt and pepper.

2. Heat the oil in a large heavy-bottomed skillet; when it is very hot, brown the lamb in batches, without crowding, over medium-high heat. As the meat browns, transfer it to a large Dutch oven.

3. Add the butter, leek, and a little salt to the pan that the meat has cooked in; cook over low heat until soft. Add the flour, cook over low heat, stirring, for 2 minutes, and then add a little of the stock, scraping up the browned bits from the bottom. Transfer to the Dutch oven; add the bouquet garni and enough stock to come to the level of the lamb. Bring to a slow simmer, cover, and cook for 1 hour, stirring occasionally. Do not let boil.

4. Add all the vegetables except the peas; cook, covered, until the meat is tender, which can take anywhere from 1-1/2 to 2 hours more. The meat is done when the tip of a knife goes through easily with no resistance. Stir in the parsley. Adjust seasonings if necessary. Discard the bouquet garni.

5. Cook the peas, covered, in simmering salted water. Drain peas and serve stew topped with the peas.

Random Ingredients Tips

When buying lamb, keep in mind that the lighter the color, the less gamey the flavor.

Leeks have a great deal of dirt and grit between their layers. To ensure that the dirt doesn't ruin your stew, chop the leeks, put in a bowl of cold water, slosh them around, and then remove them with a skimmer or slotted spoon, leaving the dirt behind. Pat dry before sautéing.

After you cut the cheesecloth for the bouquet garni, shake off any loose bits of it that remain.

Frisée and Watercress Salad with Apples and Toasted Walnuts

Cider Vinaigrette

1 1/4 teaspoons Dijon mustard

1/4 cup apple "balsamic"
(also called Bouquet de Pommes)

2 tablespoons cider vinegar

Kosher salt and freshly ground black
pepper to taste

1/4 cup hazelnut or walnut oil

1/4 cup canola or safflower oil

1 teaspoon finely chopped shallot

Salad

2 cups watercress, leaves and upper
1 inch of stems only, washed and
chilled

6 cups frisée, washed and chilled

3/4 cup coarsely chopped toasted
walnuts (toast at 300 degrees for
10 minutes)

2 Granny Smith apples, cored,
quartered and cut in thin slices

1. To make the cider vinaigrette: In a bowl, whisk together the mustard, balsamic, vinegar, salt, and pepper. Add the oils in a slow stream, whisking, until the dressing is emulsified. Stir in the shallot. The vinaigrette may be made up to one day ahead and refrigerated, covered. Bring to room temperature before serving.

2. To serve: Put the frisée and watercress in a big bowl, add salt and pepper to taste, toss with the vinaigrette, and top with the walnuts and apples.

Seasonal Ingredients Tip

Granny Smiths are available year-round; when it's apple season, substitute any tart, crisp local apple.

Vary this salad by using pears and pecans or almonds in place of the apples and walnuts, or by adding crumbled Bleu cheese or Goat cheese.

Apricot Whip

1/2 pound dried apricots

2 cups water

1 cup sugar, plus additional for coating baking dish

2-1/2 tablespoons fresh lemon juice

1 teaspoon vanilla extract

Pinch of kosher salt

Unsalted butter

7 large egg whites

1/4 teaspoon cream of tartar

Confectioners' sugar and/or whipped cream to serve

1. In a heavy saucepan, simmer the apricots, water, and 3/4 cup of the sugar, covered, until the apricots are plump and tender, about 20 minutes. Transfer the mixture to a food processor; purée until very smooth. Stir in the lemon juice, vanilla, and salt. Cool completely. (The apricot purée may be made 2 days ahead and chilled, covered; just be sure to bring to room temperature before proceeding.) Transfer purée to a large bowl.

2. Generously butter and sugar a 2-1/2- to 3-quart straight-sided soufflé or baking dish, knocking out the excess sugar. Place on a baking sheet lined with parchment, foil, or Silpat.

3. In another large bowl, use an electric mixer to beat the whites with the remaining 1/4 cup sugar and a pinch of salt until foamy. Add the cream of tartar; beat the whites until they hold stiff peaks.

4. Stir about 1/4 of the egg whites into the apricot purée to lighten it, then fold in the rest gently but thoroughly.

5. Scrape the mixture into the prepared dish and bake on the middle rack of a pre-heated 350-degree oven until puffed, golden brown, and just set in the center, about 35 to 45 minutes. Sprinkle with confectioners' sugar and serve immediately, garnished with whipped cream, if desired. You may also make this a day ahead, let it cool, and then cover and refrigerate. It is delicious served cold, alone or with ice cream or whipped cream.

INDIAN BUFFET

The style, colors, and strong flavors of Indian food were a constant fascination to Russel. For Ann's wedding reception in 1972, which took place at Dragon Rock (Russel's home), Russel served an Indian buffet that was similar to the following menu. Accompaniments of bright orange marigolds, brass platters, and aromatic spices make this buffet a captivating one.

ADVANCE PREPARATION NOTES

3 DAYS BEFORE THE BUFFET

Prepare Tomato Chutney. (This can also be done a week or so in advance.)

2 DAYS BEFORE THE BUFFET

If pressed for time, prepare the Curry (chicken or lamb may be added at this time; lobster should be added to the reheated Curry just before serving).

1 DAY BEFORE THE BUFFET

Prepare the Curry if not done earlier (chicken or lamb may be added at this time; lobster should be added to the reheated Curry just before serving).

DAY OF THE BUFFET

Prepare Basmati Rice with Coconut.

Prepare condiments (except for Tomato Chutney).

Make Mango Fool.

Add lobster to the reheated Curry just before serving.

MENU (serves 8)

Curry with Lamb, Chicken, or Lobster

Basmati Rice with Coconut

Condiments: Banana Raita, Preserved Ginger, Scallions, Tomato Chutney, Kumquats, and Green Grapes

Store-bought Pappadums

Mango Fool with Mint Leaves and Chopped Peanuts

Curry with Lamb, Chicken, or Lobster

2 tablespoons unsalted butter

2 tablespoons flour

1 Bermuda onion, finely chopped

1 green pepper, chopped

2 large celery stalks, chopped

2-1/2 cups chicken broth

3 cups chicken, lamb, or lobster (partially cooked and cut into large chunks)

1-1/2 tablespoons curry powder

3 cloves garlic, finely minced

1/2 teaspoon ground cumin

1/2 teaspoon ginger root, finely minced

Kosher salt and pepper to taste

1/2 cup raisins

Pinch of cayenne pepper

Pinch of paprika

1/3 cup heavy cream

1. Make a smooth paste of butter and flour.

2. With remaining butter, sauté onion to a very light brown.
   Add green pepper and celery. Add chicken broth, then simmer slowly.

3. Add a little bit of the broth to the flour-and-butter paste; stir into the simmering mixture with chunks of the chicken, lamb, or lobster.

4. Add the curry powder, garlic, cumin, ginger, salt, and pepper.

5. Add raisins that have been soaked for 2 hours in cold water and then drained. Season with a little cayenne and paprika.

6. Turn off the flame; add heavy cream.

NOTE: If using lamb, prepare in the following manner:

1. Melt 2 tablespoons butter or other fat in a heavy skillet.

2. Dredge the meat lightly with flour and brown on all sides.

3. Remove lamb pieces from the pan and set aside until ready to use in step 3 above.

NOTE: If using lobster, do not add until you reheat the curry mixture just before serving on the day of the party.

Curry Tip

Curry is always better the second day. Prepare the recipe the day before except for the addition of heavy cream. When ready to serve, reheat the curry, then add the cream to finish.

Basmati Rice with Coconut

2 cups basmati rice

4 cups water

1/2 cup toasted coconut

1. Rinse rice thoroughly. Bring water to a boil. Add rice and stir.

2. Bring to a boil once more, lower the heat, and cover.

3. Simmer until the water is absorbed, about 15 minutes.

4. Remove the rice from the heat and allow to stand for 5 minutes.

5. Stir lightly. Gently blend in the toasted coconut and serve.

Mango Fool with Mint Leaves and Chopped Peanuts

2 ripe round mangoes, reddish in color (berries, peaches, or bananas may be used instead)

2 tablespoons sugar

2 tablespoons fresh lime juice

Dash of kosher salt

1-1/2 cups heavy cream, very cold

1/4 cup sugar

1/2 cup chopped salted peanuts for garnish

Mint sprigs for garnish

1. Cut the mangoes top to bottom, making one cut on either side of the long pit. When you feel some resistance, you will know you've hit the pit. Separate halves and remove the pit.

2. Cut crosshatches in the flesh, going almost to the skin. With a spoon or knife, separate the cubes from the skin and put into the work bowl of a food processor.

3. Add the sugar, lime juice, and salt; process until smooth. If there are any fibrous strings (some mangoes are more fibrous than others), remove them. You should have 1-1/2 cups of purée.

4. Chill, covered, for at least 1 hour or up to one day. If you're in a hurry, freeze the purée for 20 minutes before proceeding.

5. Freeze the bowl and beaters of an electric mixer for 10 minutes or longer. Remove from freezer; add the cream and sugar to the bowl and beat to stiff peaks.

6. Mix about 1/4 of the whipped cream into the mango purée, then fold in the remaining cream gently but thoroughly. Chill for 2 to 8 hours to firm the fool slightly and to allow the flavors to meld.

7. Serve garnished with chopped peanuts and mint sprigs.

Condiments

Banana Raita

2 tablespoons slivered blanched almonds

1 cup plain yogurt

1 cup sour cream

3 to 4 tablespoons honey or sugar

1/8 teaspoon ground cardamom or grated nutmeg

1 medium-sized ripe banana, peeled and thinly sliced

1. Mix the almonds with the yogurt, sour cream, honey or sugar, and cardamom or nutmeg in a bowl.

2. Add the banana slices; gently fold them into the yogurt mixture.

3. Cover and chill thoroughly.

Preserved Ginger

Chop into small pieces.

NOTE: Preserved ginger can be purchased at most supermarkets.

Scallions

Chop into small pieces.

NOTE: Include the green stems along with the white to add color, crisp flavor, and contrast.

Tomato Chutney

1-1/2 teaspoons fresh ginger,
finely minced

1/2 teaspoons mustard seed

1/2 teaspoon turmeric

2 tablespoons vegetable oil

3 cups ripe tomatoes, finely chopped

2 cups apples, peeled and chopped

2 small onions, peeled and finely
chopped

1-1/2 teaspoons finely minced garlic

1 lemon, seeded and chopped,
including rind

2 cups cider vinegar

1 cup seedless raisins

2-1/2 cups brown sugar

1-1/2 tablespoons olive oil

1/4 teaspoon ground cloves

1 teaspoon kosher salt

1/4 teaspoon black pepper

1. Cook ginger, mustard seed, and turmeric in oil in a small skillet over low heat, stirring until the seeds begin to pop, about 2 or 3 minutes.

2. Combine with remaining ingredients in a heavy saucepan and cook over medium heat for about 1 hour, until liquid has become thick and syrupy.

   NOTE: This recipe can be made a week before. Keep covered in the refrigerator.

Kumquats

1. Slice or quarter lengthwise.

2. Cover and refrigerate until ready to use.

Green Grapes

1. Use fresh green grapes; slice.

2. Cover and refrigerate until ready to use.

DRAGON ROCK DINNER

ADVANCE PREPARATION NOTES

2 DAYS BEFORE THE DINNER

Prepare Beef Stew with Green Apples.

1 DAY BEFORE THE DINNER

Prepare Chocolate Pots de Crème.

Clean and wash greens; store in tightly closed plastic bag in refrigerator.

Prepare salad dressing.

DAY OF THE DINNER

Prepare Mashed Potatoes and Turnips.

Finish salad just before serving.

Reheat Beef Stew with Green Apples.

This dinner was a favorite for our Garrison, New York, home. Robust and warming, it seemed a natural for the country. Stews can easily be made in advance and frozen for a future dinner or, when frozen, can travel from the city to the country. The unusual addition of tart Granny Smith apples gives this beef stew a refreshing dimension.

MENU (Serves 6)

Beef Stew with Green Apples

Mashed Potatoes and Turnips

Endive and Watercress Salad with Mustard Vinaigrette

Shelley Boris's Chocolate Pots de Crème

Beef Stew with Green Apples

1-1/2 pounds beef chuck or shoulder	1/2 cup red wine
1/2 cup onion, thinly sliced	1 cup water
1 medium-size carrot, thinly sliced	Kosher salt to taste
2 celery stalks, chopped	Pepper to taste
1/2 clove garlic, minced	1/4 teaspoon Thyme
1 tablespoon parsley, finely minced	1 Bay leaf
2 tablespoons bacon drippings	2 green apples, diced

1. Cut meat into 1-inch cubes.

2. Sauté onion, carrot, celery, garlic, and parsley in bacon drippings until they are lightly browned. Add meat cubes and brown on all sides.

3. Add remaining ingredients, except for the apples; cover tightly, simmering very slowly for about 3 hours, until meat is thoroughly tender.

4. Add the green apples during the last 15 minutes of cooking time. Add more liquid during cooking if needed.

Mashed Potatoes and Turnips

2 medium turnips	1/2 cup heavy cream
4 to 5 medium potatoes	Kosher salt and pepper to taste
Salted water	1-2 cloves roasted garlic (optional)
1/2 cup unsalted butter	

1. Peel and slice turnips and potatoes.

2. Cook in boiling salted water until tender.

3. Drain and mash with butter and cream until smooth.

4. Season with salt, pepper, and roasted garlic, if using.

Endive and Watercress Salad with Mustard Vinaigrette

Dressing

2 tablespoons fresh lemon juice or balsamic vinegar

1 tablespoon honey mustard

1 small shallot, finely minced

1 clove garlic, finely minced

1/2 to 3/4 cup olive oil

Kosher salt and pepper to taste

1. Whisk together lemon juice or vinegar, honey mustard, shallot, and garlic in a small bowl.

2. Add olive oil in a small stream, whisking until emulsified. Add salt and pepper to taste.

Salad

2 heads Belgian endive

2 bunches watercress, tough stems discarded

2 small heads bibb lettuce, leaves separated

4 heads mâche (about 1/4 pound)

2 hearts of romaine lettuce, cut or torn into 2-inch pieces

1. Wash all the greens well and pat them dry.

2. Toss thoroughly but lightly with dressing and serve.

Shelley Boris's Chocolate Pots de Crème

2 cups whole milk

1 cup heavy cream

8 ounces Callebaut bittersweet chocolate, finely chopped

2 teaspoons vanilla extract

1 teaspoon coffee extract

8 large egg yolks (4 ounces)

1/2 cup sugar

Whipped cream

1. Scald the milk and cream.

2. Whisk in the chocolate and the vanilla and coffee extracts until the chocolate is melted.

3. Whisk egg yolks and sugar together in a bowl.

4. Using a whisk, temper the yolk-and-sugar mixture by slowly adding all of the chocolate mixture. (This is the most critical step—do this very carefully!)

5. Place bowl on top of a pan of boiling water (creating a double boiler). Stir mixture with a rubber scraper until the pudding is slightly thickened, until it reaches 170 degrees or about 10 minutes. Do not overcook.

6. Strain pudding through a fine sieve or chinoise; quickly pour into 4-ounce ramekins, filling to the top. Do not cover with plastic, as this will mar the surface. Instead, place a piece of heavy waxed paper over the ramekins, then the plastic. Chill until set.

7. Serve cold with freshly whipped cream and a dusting of shaved chocolate.

NOTE: Coffee extract is available from:

The Baker's Catalogue
Norwich, Vermont
(800) 827–6836 phone
(800) 343–3002 fax
bakerscatalogue.com

SOUTHERN DINNER FOR WINTER

ADVANCE PREPARATION NOTES

1 OR 2 DAYS BEFORE THE DINNER

Make turnover filling; refrigerate.

Make turnover dough, divide, and let rest; roll out and freeze.

Make Brunswick Stew.

DAY OF THE DINNER

Cook greens in ham stock before guests arrive; sauté just before serving.

Fill and bake turnovers before guests arrive; reheat to serve.

Make Spoon Bread while reheating stew or before guests arrive. Reheat if necessary.

Traditionally made with squirrel, Brunswick stew these days is often made with chicken or rabbit. Russel liked it with chicken and ham, accompanied with spoon bread made from a recipe given to him by an Alabaman. It is also good with rice or buttermilk biscuits. We used Arkansas peppered ham sliced off the bone, but it works well with any flavorful ham, such as Black Forest. Try to avoid using the boiled, cold-cut–type ham.

MENU (serves 8)

Brunswick Stew

Sautéed Greens with Ham Hock

Spoon Bread

Pear-Ginger Turnovers

Brunswick Stew

2 tablespoons unsalted butter

1 cup diced country ham

3 cups diced Spanish onion

2/3 cup diced carrot

2 thyme sprigs

Salt and freshly ground black pepper
to taste

1 tablespoon minced garlic

5 pounds skin-on chicken thighs
and breasts

Wondra flour to coat chicken

Canola, grapeseed, or safflower oil
to coat pan

3 cups chicken broth

2 cups canned chopped tomatoes

1 bay leaf

1 teaspoon dried sage leaves

1/4 teaspoon Worcestershire sauce

3 tablespoons chopped flat-leaf
parsley

2 cups baby lima beans, defrosted
if frozen

2 cups corn kernels, defrosted
if frozen

1 tablespoon grated lemon zest

1 tablespoon fresh lemon juice

Hot sauce to taste

3 tablespoons chopped chives for
garnish

Wondra Tip

Wondra, finely milled white flour available in supermarkets, is ideal for this stew and any other dish for which a light coating is desired, such as sautéed fish fillets, scallops, chicken, or veal cutlets.

1. Heat the butter in a large heavy-bottomed skillet, and when the foam subsides, add the ham. Cook over low heat for 3 minutes. Remove with a slotted spoon and put in a Dutch oven that is large enough to cook the stew in.

2. Add the onion, carrot, thyme, salt, and pepper to the skillet; cook until the vegetables are tender and pale gold. Add the garlic and cook for a few seconds longer, just until it becomes fragrant. Remove the vegetables and add to the Dutch oven.

3. Heat enough oil to film the bottom of the skillet; when the oil is hot, add the chicken pieces, skin-side-down, in a single layer without crowding; cook over medium heat until golden brown on all sides (to avoid crowding, fry in several batches). Transfer the chicken to the Dutch oven as you finish each batch.

4. When all the chicken has browned, pour off the fat and add the broth to the skillet; cook, stirring to get all the browned bits up from the bottom. Pour into the Dutch oven, add the tomatoes, bay leaf, sage, and Worcestershire sauce, plus additional salt and pepper; bring to a simmer and cook 30 to 45 minutes, stirring occasionally. Add the parsley, lima beans, corn, and lemon zest during the last 15 minutes. The chicken is done when its juices run clear, without a trace of pink; the breasts may take a bit less time than the thighs.

5. Remove the chicken. Let the sauce reduce over medium heat until it thickens to the consistency of a thin gravy, about 3 minutes. When the chicken is cool enough to handle, remove the skin and bones, and tear the meat into large shreds. Return to the Dutch oven; heat through.

6. Just before serving, stir in the lemon juice and hot sauce, and top with the chives.

Sautéed Greens with Ham Hock

2 smoked ham hocks

1/2 habanero chili, seeds removed

**One yellow onion, peeled and halved
  lengthwise, root end trimmed but
  left attached**

**5 pounds assorted braising greens, such
  as chard, collards, kale (Tuscan kale,
  also known as dragon kale or lacinato,
  is particularly tasty), dandelions,
  turnips, or beet or mustard greens**

**Kosher salt and freshly ground
  black pepper to taste**

Bacon fat for sautéing

3/4 teaspoon finely minced garlic

1. First make a broth by combining 5 quarts cold water with the ham hocks, habanero, onion, and a few tablespoons of salt in a large pot. Bring to boil, cover, and cook on low heat for 1 hour.

2. Trim and then wash the greens (this can be done the day before to save time and refrigerator space, or while you wait for the water to come to a boil). Strip the leaves from the stems by holding the stem in one hand and pulling the leaves off from top to bottom with the other. Tear the greens into the same size pieces as you would for salad; rinse well. Discard the stems.

3. Remove the habanero, hocks, and onion from the broth and discard. Increase the heat to high. Add the greens to the broth, stirring with a wire skimmer or long spoon so they will start shrinking to fit in the pot. Cook until tender, about 15 minutes. Drain in a colander. (The recipe can be prepared ahead up to this point; if you plan to sauté the greens later, run cold water over them to stop the cooking and press most of the water out with the back of a spoon or skimmer. Refrigerate if you plan to wait more than 2 hours to sauté them.)

4. When you are ready to sauté the greens, warm enough bacon fat (duck fat is also excellent) to film the bottom of a large skillet. Add the greens and adjust the seasoning; cook over low heat, stirring occasionally, until they have a buttery texture and have lost their bitter edge, about 25 minutes. Add the garlic about 5 minutes before the greens are done.

Spoon Bread

1 quart milk

2 teaspoons kosher salt

1 teaspoon sugar (optional)

1 cup cornmeal

3 tablespoons unsalted butter

Freshly ground black pepper to taste

4 large eggs, separated

1 teaspoon baking powder

1. Combine the milk, salt, and sugar in a heavy-bottomed saucepan.

2. Bring the milk to a simmer, stirring often to keep the bottom from scorching. Add the cornmeal in a thin stream, whisking constantly to keep it from lumping. Reduce the heat to low once all the cornmeal has been added. Cook until thick, stirring almost constantly, about 10 minutes. When you lift the spoon and let the mixture fall back into the pot, it should form a slowly dissolving ribbon. Remove from the heat and add the butter and pepper. Add the egg yolks one at a time, stirring after each addition to blend thoroughly.

3. Beat the egg whites with a pinch of salt until stiff but not dry; add about half a cup to the cornmeal mixture, which will loosen it up and make it easier to incorporate the beaten egg whites.

4. Add the whites to the cornmeal mixture, along with the baking powder; fold until the whites are fairly evenly blended in. A few small pockets of white are fine.

5. Transfer to a buttered baking dish (about the size of a lasagna pan) set on a baking sheet; cook in a preheated 350-degree oven until the top has some cracks and the center looks jiggly but not wet, about 20 minutes. Serve warm.

Pear-Ginger Turnovers

These turnovers are delicate and flaky in texture, not like the tough, thick ones most of us are used to. The ginger, cardamom, and pepper in the filling enhance the pears' natural flavor without overwhelming them.

Turnover Dough

2 cups all-purpose flour

14 tablespoons frozen unsalted butter, cut into small pieces

4 teaspoons sugar

1/4 teaspoon kosher salt

4 to 6 tablespoons ice water

Filling

2-1/2 pounds firm ripe pears, such as Comice or Bosc

Juice of 1 lemon

Dash of kosher salt

4 tablespoons unsalted butter

1/4 cup sugar

1 teaspoon finely grated fresh ginger root

1/4 teaspoon ground cardamom

1/8 teaspoon freshly ground black pepper

To finish

Heavy cream

Sugar

Make the dough

1. Combine the flour, butter, sugar, and salt in the work bowl of a food processor; pulse about eight times, or until the butter pieces are the size of large peas. Add 2 tablespoons of the water, sprinkling it over the flour mixture; process for 3 seconds.

2. Transfer to a lightly floured surface. If the dough seems dry, add a little more water, just enough to hold it together when pressed. Toss the mixture with your hands to incorporate the water, then blend by pushing the dough down and away from you with the heels of your hands, working in sections. Streaks or pieces of the butter should still be visible. If the butter starts to get too soft, transfer the mixture to a bowl or baking sheet and put in the freezer for a few minutes to firm it up.

3. Divide the dough into 8 equal pieces. Form into disks, flatten slightly, and cover with plastic wrap. Refrigerate for a minimum of 1 hour, or overnight. (The dough freezes well.)

4. Roll each disk out into a 6-inch circle; refrigerate for 30 minutes or longer.

Make the filling

Peel, quarter, and core the pears. Cut the quarters into 1/4-inch-thick slices. Toss in a bowl with the lemon juice and salt. Heat the butter to bubbling in a large skillet and add as many pears as you can without crowding them. They should sauté rather than steam. The sautéing may have to be done in two batches. Add the sugar, ginger, cardamom and pepper; cook over high heat, stirring occasionally, until the juices become syrupy, about 2 minutes. Don't let them cook too long or they will turn to mush. Spread the pears out on a baking sheet and let them cool completely.

Make the turnovers

1. Line a baking sheet with Silpat (ideal) or buttered parchment paper. When the dough and filling have chilled, form the turnovers on the baking sheet: Making sure that the dough is cold but pliable, put 1/8 of the filling on the lower half of each circle, leaving about an inch of border on the bottom and two sides. Fold in half so that the edges meet, press out any air, and with the tines of a floured fork, press to seal, making a little border. Brush with cream and sprinkle each turnover with 1 teaspoon of sugar. Prick the top 3 times with a fork to let the steam out. If the dough or formed turnovers get too soft as you work, return them to the freezer for a few minutes.

2. Bake on the lower-middle rack of a preheated 425-degree oven for 10 minutes, then move to the top rack for the remaining 10 to 15 minutes. Let the turnovers sit for about 5 minutes before removing from the pan. Serve warm (reheating is fine).

CHRISTMAS BUFFET

ADVANCE PREPARATION NOTES

3 DAYS BEFORE THE BUFFET

Prepare pie dough. (Note: If you decide to do this in advance, if you carefully wrap the dough in plastic wrap and foil so you can freeze it.)

2 DAYS BEFORE THE BUFFET

Complete first two steps of Chicken Fricassee recipe.

1 DAY BEFORE THE BUFFET

Prepare Lemon Pudding; refrigerate tightly covered.

DAY OF BUFFET

Prepare Braised Fennel. Finish Chicken Fricassee. Finish salad.

Our small family eagerly anticipated Christmas and all the festivities that accompany this very busy time of the year. Company was welcomed and Russel, very theatrical in nature, loved to decorate our home and table. Most of this menu can be made a day or two in advance and reheated, except of course, the completion of the grapefruit salad and those delicious dumplings!

MENU (serves 8)

Chicken Fricassee with Egg Dumplings and Peas

Braised Fennel

Avocado and Grapefruit Salad

Lemon Pudding

White Christmas Pie

Chicken Fricassee with Egg Dumplings and Peas

Fricassee

1 plump stewing hen

2 pounds veal shoulder

1 carrot, roughly chopped

1 bay leaf

2 medium white onions, thinly sliced

1 tablespoon finely chopped tarragon,
chives, and parsley

Freshly grated nutmeg to taste

Kosher salt and pepper to taste

4 tablespoons unsalted butter

2 tablespoons flour

2 large egg yolks

3 to 4 tablespoons sherry

1 pound mushrooms, thinly sliced

1-1/2 cups peas (frozen is fine)

Dumplings

1 cup cake flour

1 level teaspoon baking powder

1/2 teaspoon kosher salt

1 large egg, broken into measuring cup

Milk (enough to fill same cup half full)

1 tablespoon finely chopped parsley

1. For a rich broth, cook together in a fairly small amount of water hen and veal shoulder, carrot, and a bay leaf. When tender, remove the chicken from the bone and cut into good-sized pieces. Cut the veal the same way. Set the meat aside.

2. Sauté the onions in 1 tablespoon of butter; add to simmering broth along with seasonings. Cook until the broth has reduced somewhat and is more concentrated.

   NOTE: Cook the dumplings before thickening the broth. It may not need thickening, as dumplings may concentrate the juice, and the egg will thicken it enough.

3. To make the dumplings, sift the flour three times with baking powder and salt. Beat the egg and milk together until foamy.

4. Then get the broth bubbling hot. Just 10 to 12 minutes before fricassee is to be served, mix the egg/milk mixture into the flour, baking powder, and salt mixture with a few light rapid strokes, keeping the batter as stiff as possible. Add remaining tablespoon of parsley to the dumpling batter. Drop by spoonfuls into the hot broth. Cook the dumplings 10 minutes uncovered, then cover and cook approximately 10 minutes more until done. Remove dumplings with a slotted spoon and set aside.

5. Thicken the broth if necessary. Add 2 tablespoons of butter mixed thoroughly with 2 tablespoons of flour; bring to a boil. Salt to taste and reduce the heat. Add 2 egg yolks to which a small amount of hot broth has been added to prevent curdling. Cook a few minutes more. Add sherry 1 tablespoon at a time until the flavor is rich, but without the sherry being noticeable.

6. Sauté mushrooms in the remaining tablespoon of butter and add to the sauce along with the peas; cook until done.

7. Combine all ingredients gently and serve immediately.

Braised Fennel

4 heads of fennel

8 tablespoons unsalted butter

1 medium onion, finely chopped

1 clove garlic, minced

2 cups chicken broth

Kosher salt and freshly ground black pepper to taste

1 tablespoon lemon juice

2 tablespoons chopped chives

Freshly grated orange zest (optional)

1. Trim the fennel so that just the bottom bulbs remain and remove any outer layers that are tough, stringy, or discolored. Then cut the fennel bulbs into quarters.

2. Melt the butter in a heavy skillet and add the onion and garlic; cook for 1 to 2 minutes. Add the fennel quarters and brown them lightly on all sides.

3. Add the chicken broth, and simmer, covered, for approximately 30 to 40 minutes, or until fennel is tender when pierced with a knife.

4. Season with salt and freshly ground black pepper to taste, then remove the fennel from the skillet. Add lemon juice to the remaining liquid.

5. Reduce the remaining liquid by about half, or until it is thick, and pour over the fennel again. Sprinkle the chopped chives and orange zest over the top.

Avocado and Grapefruit Salad

2 grapefruits

3 medium-to-large ripe avocados

Lettuce leaves

Lemon juice

Olive oil

Kosher salt and freshly ground black pepper to taste

1. Peel grapefruit so that white skin is completely removed. With a sharp knife, remove sections of the grapefruit, each in one piece.

2. Combine grapefruit sections with slices of avocado.

3. Serve on lettuce with a citrus dressing made of 1 part lemon juice, 2 parts olive oil, salt, and pepper.

Lemon Pudding

1 heaping tablespoon flour

1 cup sugar

1 cup milk

3 large egg yolks, beaten

1 tablespoon melted unsalted butter

Juice of 2 lemons

Grated zest of 1 lemon

Pinch of kosher salt

3 egg whites, stiffly beaten

1. Mix flour with sugar. Add milk and stir.
2. Stir in egg yolks, butter, lemon juice, lemon zest, and salt.
3. Fold in egg whites.
4. Place in buttered baking dish (2-quart capacity) and set in a shallow pan of hot water.
5. Bake 30 to 40 minutes in a 350-degree preheated oven.
6. Serve either hot or cold.

White Christmas Pie

Pie Shell

1 cup all-purpose flour

7 tablespoons frozen unsalted butter, cut into small pieces

2 teaspoons sugar

1/8 teaspoon kosher salt

2 to 3 tablespoons ice water

Pie Filling

1 envelope gelatin

1/2 cup cold water

1/4 cup flour

1/2 cup sugar

1/2 teaspoon kosher salt

1-1/4 cups milk

1 teaspoon vanilla extract

1/4 teaspoon almond extract

1/2 cup whipped cream

3 large egg whites

1/4 teaspoon cream of tartar

1/2 cup sugar

1 cup moist shredded coconut

Toasted almonds for garnish

To make pie shell

1. Combine the flour, butter, sugar, and salt in the work bowl of a food processor; pulse about eight times, or until the butter pieces are the size of large peas.

2. Add 2 tablespoons of ice water, sprinkling it over the flour mixture; process for 3 seconds.

3. Transfer to a lightly floured surface. If the dough seems dry, add a little more water, just enough to hold it together when pressed.

4. Toss the mixture with your hands to incorporate the water, then blend by pushing the dough down and away from you with the heels of your hands, working in sections. Streaks or pieces of the butter should still be visible.

5. Form into a thick disk, cover with plastic wrap, and flatten a bit more. Refrigerate for a minimum of 1 hour, or overnight (the dough freezes well).

6. Before rolling out the dough, let it sit for 5 minutes, then roll it into an 11- or 12-inch circle. Transfer to a baking sheet, cover with plastic wrap, and chill for 10 minutes or so, until firm.

7. Preheat oven to 375 degrees.

8. Line a tart shell with rolled-out dough, then line with waxed paper and dried beans; bake for 10 to 15 minutes, or until dough is set.

9. Remove beans and waxed paper and continue to bake for approximately another 5 minutes.

To make pie filling

1. Soften gelatin in 1/2 cup cold water.

2. Mix flour, sugar, and salt together in a saucepan, then add milk, stirring well. Cook over a low heat, stirring constantly until sugar is completely dissolved. Raise heat to medium and boil 1 minute. Remove from heat and stir in softened gelatin. Chill. When partially set, beat with rotary beater or wire whisk until smooth.

3. Add vanilla and almond extracts, then fold in the whipped cream.

4. Beat egg whites, cream of tartar, and sugar into a meringue; then fold into above mixture.

5. Fold in coconut and pile into cooled, baked pie shell.

6. Sprinkle top with coconut, then chill about 2 hours.

7. Take chilled pie out of refrigerator 20 minutes before serving so crust will crisp a bit. Sprinkle a few toasted almonds on top.

CHINESE NEW YEAR

ADVANCE PREPARATION NOTES

Margaret Spader's Chinese Spiced Walnuts can be made 2 months in advance if they are kept in the refrigerator in a tightly sealed container.

1 OR 2 DAYS BEFORE

Complete first three steps of Chrysanthemum Duckling recipe.

Cut bread slices for Scallop Toasts.

Make salad dressing.

Wash bok choy or lettuce and keep in refrigerator in paper towels placed in a closed plastic bag.

(Most Chinese cooking requires that preparation be done on the day of your dinner, but it is always worth it.)

Under the adept tutelage of Margaret Spader, Russel discovered that even though Chinese food in its presentation was not as visual to him as other cuisines, it more than made up for this in flavor. The Chrysanthemum Duckling was his attempt to add theatre and beauty to this great array of colors and flavors. As a child, breaking off the petals of the chrysanthemum into the piping hot duck was my very favorite job at parties.

MENU (serves 8)

Margaret Spader's Chinese Spiced Walnuts

Scallop Toast

Chrysanthemum Duckling

Jasmine Rice

Korean Salad

Lime Sorbet with Shredded Coconut and Orange

Store-bought Fortune Cookies

Margaret Spader's Chinese Spiced Walnuts

6 cups water

4 cups walnut halves

1/2 cup sugar

1 teaspoon hot pepper flakes

2 cups salad oil (approximately)

Kosher salt to taste

1. Bring water to a boil in a 2-quart heavy saucepan, add the walnuts, and reheat to boiling; cook 1 to 2 minutes. Drain in a colander or large sieve, rinse under hot running water, and shake the colander to drain well.

2. Turn the walnuts into a bowl, add the sugar and pepper flakes, and toss to coat the nuts.

3. In a heavy-bottomed saucepan or electric skillet, heat the oil to 350 degrees. (The oil should be about 1 inch deep.) Add about half the walnuts; stirring occasionally, fry until golden brown, about 5 minutes. Remove the walnuts with a slotted spoon. Drain on a cloth towel (do not use a paper towel as the hot nuts have a tendency to stick), or place the nuts in a sieve over a deep bowl so the oil will drain off.

4. Sprinkle lightly with salt; toss gently to keep the nuts from sticking together.

5. Fry the remaining walnuts. Tightly covered, these nuts will keep for 1 to 2 months in the refrigerator. Makes 4-1/2 cups.

Scallop Toast

1 pound fresh scallops
(or 1/2 pound of scallops and 1/2 pound of fresh fillet or finely minced pork)

4 tablespoons finely chopped pork

8 water chestnuts

2 tablespoons dry sherry

2 teaspoons kosher salt

2 large eggs, lightly beaten

3 tablespoons cornstarch

12 thin slices white bread (3 to 4 days old for a crisp toast)

3 cups peanut oil

Toasted sesame seeds for garnish

1. Wash the scallops and pat dry. Finely mince the pork and mix with the scallops.

2. Peel and wash the water chestnuts. Chop fine and add to the scallop mixture.

3. Add sherry, salt, eggs, and cornstarch to the scallop mixture; mix well.

4. Remove crusts from bread slices and cut each slice into 4 squares or triangles.

5. Spoon a mound of the scallop mixture over each bread slice. Smooth over the tops.

6. Heat the oil to 375 degrees. Lower in the pieces of bread, scallop side down. Fry 4 to 5 pieces one at a time. Fry one minute, then turn and fry until golden brown.

7. Drain on paper towels and serve piping hot.

8. Add toasted sesame seeds for garnish. Makes 48 pieces.

Chrysanthemum Duckling

6 cups chicken broth

2 (5-pound) ducks, quartered

1/4 cup peanut oil

1 large green pepper cut into 1- to 2-inch pieces (same size as pineapple chunks)

1/4 cup cornstarch

1/4 cup soy sauce

1 teaspoon finely minced fresh ginger

2 tablespoons sherry

2 teaspoons finely minced garlic

3/4 cup pineapple juice

1/2 teaspoon mustard seed

Pepper to taste

3 cups fresh pineapple, cut into 1- to 2-inch chunks (same size as green pepper chunks)

40 snow peas

1/2 cup finely chopped scallions

1 large chrysanthemum flower

1. Bring chicken broth to a boil and add the duck quarters.

2. Simmer on low heat for 45 minutes. Turn off the flame and leave the duck in the broth for 15 minutes. Remove the pieces and cool. Set the broth in a cool place so that the fat will come to the top.

3. Remove the fat and bone from the duck (leave the skin on), keeping the meat in 2-inch pieces.

4. Heat the oil in a skillet; brown the duck pieces on all sides. Put the pieces in a shallow pan and keep warm until serving time. They should be crisp on the outside when added to the sauce.

5. Sauté the pieces of pepper very lightly. These should also be crisp and not soft. Set aside.

6. Mix cornstarch, soy sauce, ginger, sherry, and garlic together in a bowl. Set aside.

7. Add pineapple juice, broth, sherry mixture, and mustard seeds to the skillet; bring to a boil, adding soy sauce (instead of salt) and pepper to taste. If more thickening is needed, add 1 to 2 tablespoons more of cornstarch to the sauce.

8. Just before serving, add the pineapple chunks, snow peas, and green pepper; bring to a boil. Sprinkle in chopped scallions. Do not overcook.

9. Place the chrysanthemum in a bowl adjacent to the duck; at the table or just before serving, break off petals and scatter over the duck.

Jasmine Rice

2 cups jasmine rice

4 cups water

1 teaspoon kosher salt

1 tablespoon unsalted butter or oil

1. Rinse rice well.
2. Bring water, salt, and butter to a boil, then add rice.
3. Lower heat and cover; cook for 15 minutes or until done.
4. Fluff and serve.

Korean Salad

Dressing

1/4 cup sesame seeds

1 teaspoon chili peppers, crushed

1/2 cup salad oil

1/4 cup red wine vinegar

1/4 cup soy sauce

1. Parch the sesame seeds and chili peppers in a medium hot frying pan until the seeds are brown and have absorbed most of the peppery heat of the chili peppers.
2. Combine salad oil, wine vinegar, and soy sauce.

   NOTE: Soy sauce can be very salty, so try less at first, then adjust.

Salad

2 heads Chinese cabbage, also known as Napa cabbage, or an equivalent amount of bok choy. Romaine makes a good substitute.

1. Wash the greens well and pat dry.
2. Break them up into bite-size pieces.
3. Toss lightly with dressing.
4. Sprinkle the top of the salad mixture with the sesame seeds and chili peppers. Serve.

Bok Choy Tip

Bok choy is available in Chinese groceries all year round. It will keep for a week in the refrigerator if it is wrapped in a plastic bag.

Lime Sorbet with Shredded Coconut and Orange

2 to 3 oranges

Lime sorbet, store-bought

1/2 to 3/4 cup shredded coconut

1. With a sharp knife, cut the bottom or top ends off an orange so it can lie flat. Remove the skin and pith by cutting down the orange from top to bottom, working your way around and trying to keep the shape of the fruit as you go.

2. Holding the fruit in your hand, cut out the sections by inserting the knife right next to each side of each membrane and cutting down.

3. When ready to serve, sprinkle shredded coconut over individual servings of orange sections and sorbet.

GERMAN DINNER FOR A COLD NIGHT

ADVANCE PREPARATION NOTES

2 DAYS BEFORE THE DINNER

Make Apple Strudel filling.

Marinate beef for Sauerbraten.

1 DAY BEFORE THE DINNER

Make Apple Strudel filling (if not done earlier).

Cook Sauerbraten.

Defrost phyllo in refrigerator.

Make Cucumber Salad.

Make bread crumbs for broccoli.

Wash and cut broccoli. You may also cook it through step 2 of the recipe.

DAY OF THE DINNER

Make Apple Strudel filling (if not done earlier).

Make Potato Kugel before dinner; reheat if necessary.

Fill and bake strudel.

Boil the broccoli.

Remove fat from Sauerbraten. Reheat Sauerbraten; let the meat rest 10 to 15 minutes while you reduce the pan liquid.

Sauté broccoli while Sauerbraten is resting.

Slice Sauerbraten.

Since both our fathers loved German food, we frequently went to Luchow's, a fancy German restaurant on 14th street in Manhattan that was a popular place for dinner in the 1950s and '60s. It was a treat to go there for sauerbraten, roast goose, and crêpes suzette. German food has fallen out of favor since then, but we still love it for its hearty flavors and the memories it evokes.

MENU (serves 8)

Sauerbraten

Potato Kugel

Broccoli with Browned Bread Crumbs

Dilled Cucumber Salad

Warm Apple Strudel with Dulce de Leche Ice Cream

Sauerbraten

Many recipes, including Russel's original one, call for marinating the meat for up to 10 days. We find that marinating for more than 1 or 2 days makes the meat too sour for our taste. We prefer it with a pleasant balance of sweet and sour flavors.

Meat and marinade

4 pounds boneless chuck roast, rolled and tied

3 cups red wine (we used a $10 pinot noir from Chile)

1/2 cup red wine vinegar

2 bay leaves

4 cloves

10 black peppercorns

2 sprigs fresh thyme

1 whole allspice

Stew ingredients

Oil to film pan

4 cups thinly sliced Spanish onion

1/4 cup chopped carrot

1/4 cup chopped celery

2 sprigs fresh thyme

Kosher salt and freshly ground black pepper

1 tablespoon minced garlic

Wondra flour to lightly coat meat

6 tablespoons tomato paste

1/2 cup raisins

3 tablespoons dark brown sugar

3 tablespoons chopped celery leaves for garnish

Sour cream for serving (optional)

1. Put the meat into a nonreactive container. Combine the marinade ingredients and pour over the meat; cover and refrigerate for 1 to 2 days.

2. Film the bottom of a heavy Dutch oven with oil and add the onion, carrot, celery, thyme, salt, and pepper. Cook over medium-low heat until tender. Add the garlic and cook for a few seconds longer. Transfer to a bowl or the upside-down lid of the Dutch oven.

3. Remove the meat from the marinade. Strain the marinade and reserve. Dry the meat with paper towels, season with salt and pepper, and lightly coat with Wondra flour.

4. Add more oil to the Dutch oven; when it is hot, brown the meat on all sides over medium heat, lowering the heat if necessary so that the flour doesn't burn. Remove the meat and pour off any excess fat.

5. Add the marinade to the pan and cook over high heat, scraping up the browned bits from the bottom, until it boils for a minute or two. Return the meat and vegetables to the pan and add the tomato paste, raisins, brown sugar, and additional salt and pepper.

6. Reduce the heat to very low, cover, and cook about 4 hours, or until a skewer inserted into the meat goes through without resistance. Turn the meat over halfway through cooking and adjust the heat as necessary to keep the liquid at a slow simmer.

7. Remove the thyme sprigs, cool the stew, then cover and refrigerate.

8. Before reheating, remove the solidified fat from the top. Cover the pot and simmer until the stew is heated through (test the meat with a metal skewer). Remove the meat, cover with foil, and let it rest for 10 to 15 minutes while finishing the sauce.

9. Simmer the pan juices until slightly thickened, about 10 minutes, stirring every now and then to make sure that nothing is sticking to the bottom.

10. Cut the meat in 1/4-inch-thick slices, spoon the sauce over, and garnish with celery leaves and sour cream, if desired.

Potato Kugel

Kugel is the German and Yiddish word for "pudding," and potato kugel is a much-loved Jewish comfort food, despite the fact that it is usually dense and leaden. This version, which contains baking powder and baking soda, is fluffy and tender inside, crisp and brown outside. We've also taken some liberties with the shape of the kugel; it's usually baked in a square or rectangular dish and cut into squares for serving. We bake ours in a round springform pan; when the sides of the pan are removed after baking, the kugel can be presented whole or cut into wedges. Potato kugel makes a great accompaniment for just about any kind of roasted or stewed meat or poultry.

3 large eggs

2 tablespoons finely chopped flat-leaf parsley

2-1/2 pounds russet potatoes

Half of a 1-1/4-pound Spanish onion, peeled, ends trimmed

1/4 cup flour

4 teaspoons baking powder

1/2 teaspoon baking soda

1-1/2 tablespoons kosher salt

Freshly ground black pepper to taste

4 tablespoons unsalted butter, melted

1. Beat the eggs in a small bowl; add the parsley and set aside.

2. Peel the potatoes; put into a bowl and cover with cold water. This will keep them from discoloring.

3. Using the large-holed side of a box grater or a food processor fitted with the coarse shredding blade, grate the potatoes alternately with the onion, doing about half a potato, then some onion, and so on, until you have used up both (the onion juices will keep the potato from discoloring). Squeeze the watery liquid out of the potato mixture and put the mixture into a bowl as you go.

4. Sift the flour, baking powder, baking soda, salt and pepper over the potato mixture; toss with your hands to combine. Add the egg mixture and the butter; stir well.

5. Transfer the mixture to an 8- or 9-inch springform pan (preferably nonstick) that has been coated with nonstick cooking spray. Smooth the top with a spatula or knife. Set the springform on a baking sheet (this helps to keep it stable on the oven rack and makes moving it much easier).

6. Bake in a preheated 400-degree oven until the top is golden, about 45 minutes.

Broccoli with Browned Bread Crumbs

The technique of cooking the broccoli in boiling water and then reheating it is ideal for entertaining (or even for simple family meals) and can be used with just about any vegetable. Restaurants do it all the time to save last-minute stress and mess. This recipe tastes best when the broccoli is tender, but to apply this technique to other vegetables, cook them until crisp-tender and reheat in a skillet with butter or oil. This also makes a great "sauce" for orecchiette or penne, with grated Parmesan or pecorino Romano mixed in.

2 slices white bread, crusts removed

1 pound broccoli

2 tablespoons olive oil

2 tablespoons unsalted butter

1 medium garlic clove, peeled and sliced thin

Kosher salt and freshly ground black pepper to taste

1. Process the bread in a food processor until it becomes coarse crumbs. Lay out on a plate or baking sheet to dry out. This will take anywhere from several hours to a day, but timing is not crucial; simply make this a day or even a week ahead of time and store in a plastic bag or covered container.

2. Cut the broccoli into florets. Cook in a large pot of rapidly boiling salted water until it is almost tender, about 2 minutes. Drain in a colander and cool under running water. (If you won't be serving the broccoli for several hours or until the next day, layer it between paper towels, store in a plastic bag, and refrigerate until you are ready for the next step.)

3. Put the oil, butter and garlic in a skillet that will be large enough to hold the broccoli in one or two layers. Warm over low heat until the garlic is fragrant but not colored. Add 1/2 cup bread crumbs (save any left over for another use), turn the heat to medium and sauté until the crumbs turn light golden. Add the broccoli, salt, and pepper, and cook until hot.

Dilled Cucumber Salad

2 English (seedless) cucumbers

1 tablespoon kosher salt

7-1/2 teaspoons sugar

6 tablespoons rice wine vinegar

2 tablespoons finely chopped fresh dill

Freshly ground black pepper to taste

1. Halve the cucumbers lengthwise and remove the seeds with a small spoon. Cut in thin slices and put in a colander. Toss with the salt, cover with wax paper or plastic wrap, and weight down with a heavy can or something similar. Let sit for 30 minutes or longer, then rinse off the salt and squeeze out as much liquid as you can without damaging the cucumbers.

2. Whisk together the remaining ingredients, making sure to dissolve the sugar, and mix with the cucumbers. Cover and chill. This is best made the day before, or at least 4 hours in advance.

Warm Apple Strudel with Dulce de Leche Ice Cream

Making apple strudel is easier than making a jelly roll. If you can, get handmade strudel dough or phyllo from a bakery. Otherwise, of the various brands available frozen in supermarkets, we prefer Kontos, which is made in New Jersey. It is less prone to tearing and drying out than the others we've tried. Defrost phyllo in the refrigerator a day before using it. Vary this recipe by substituting pears, quince, cherries, peaches, plums, or apricots for the apples (a combination of fresh and dried fruit, such as currants or dried cranberries, is also nice) and using other types of nuts.

Filling

1-1/2 pounds crisp tart apples (we used a combination of Golden Delicious, Granny Smith, and Fuji)

Juice of 1 lemon

Dash of kosher salt

4 tablespoons unsalted butter

1/4 cup Demerara sugar (see "Tip")

10 gratings of whole nutmeg

1 teaspoon vanilla extract

Strudel

1/2 pound phyllo, defrosted

4 tablespoons unsalted butter, melted

1/2 cup toasted homemade bread crumbs (from 1 slice of bread)

1/4 cup finely chopped toasted walnuts

2 tablespoons Demerara sugar

Confectioners' sugar for serving

Dulce de leche or vanilla ice cream for serving (optional)

1. Peel, core, and quarter the apples, then cut the quarters into 1/8-inch-thick slices. Toss in a bowl with the lemon juice and salt.

2. Heat the butter to bubbling in a large skillet. When the foam subsides, add as many apples as you can without crowding them. They should sauté rather than steam. The sautéing may have to be done in two batches. Cook, stirring occasionally, over medium-high heat until the apples start to wilt, about 2 minutes. Add the sugar and reduce the heat to medium. Cook until the apples are tender and their juices become syrupy, about 3 minutes. Stir in the nutmeg and vanilla. Spread the apples out on a baking sheet and let them cool completely (this may be done up to 2 days in advance).

3. Open the package of phyllo, unroll it, and put it on a baking sheet or flat surface. Cover with a damp towel or plastic wrap to keep it from drying out; keep it covered as you work. Put one sheet of phyllo on foil on a 14 x 17-inch (or similar size) baking sheet, keeping the short end closest to you. Brush with melted butter, sprinkle with the bread crumbs and nuts. Repeat with 5 more sheets of phyllo. Lay the apples on the phyllo at the end closest to you, leaving a 2-inch border on the bottom and a 1-inch border on the right and left sides. Pull the bottom over the apples, tuck the sides in, and roll up like a jelly roll, using the foil to help you lift if you need to. Make sure that the seam is on the bottom. Brush the top with the remaining butter, sprinkle with the sugar, and make about 5 diagonal slits on the top to allow steam to escape.

4. Bake in a preheated 350-degree oven until crisp and golden, about 30 to 35 minutes. Let it sit for a few minutes before dusting with confectioners' sugar and cutting into diagonal slices. Serve warm, plain or with dulce de leche or vanilla ice cream.

Sugar Tip

Demerara sugar (similar to Sugar in the Raw or turbinado sugar) is a coarse-grained light brown sugar popular in the U.K. It is available at gourmet and health-food stores and markets. It has less of a "brown" flavor and a crunchier texture than brown sugar.

AMERICAN CASUAL DINNER

ADVANCE PREPARATION NOTES

2 DAYS BEFORE THE DINNER

Finely chop black walnuts. Refrigerate in closed container.

Crumb zwieback toasts. Refrigerate in closed container.

1 DAY BEFORE THE DINNER

Complete the Black Walnut Cake.

Prepare onion, garlic, peppers, and shrimp for Shrimp Creole. Refrigerate in closed container.

DAY OF THE DINNER

Cook rice.

Prepare Shrimp Creole.

Prepare Sugar Snap Peas and Baby Yellow Pattypan Squash with Chives.

The fabled Southern hospitality is evident in this menu. Traditionally coming under the heading of "swamp cooking," this easy creole is anything but rustic today. To blend the flavors, the liquid and vegetables are
generally simmered together first, with the shrimp added only long enough to cook through. This recipe is both straightforward and stylish at the same time. Russel's friends, the Harshmans from Indiana, first introduced us to black walnuts when I was twenty years old, and I have been hooked ever since. Cooking seems to enhance their flavor, which is unlike that of any other walnuts.

MENU (serves 6)

Shrimp Creole

Popcorn Rice or White Rice

Sugar Snap Peas and Baby Yellow Pattypan Squash with Chives

Buttermilk Biscuits

Black Walnut Cake

Shrimp Creole

1/4 cup unsalted butter

2 medium onions, finely chopped

3 garlic cloves, minced

3 green peppers, coarsely chopped

1 can (28 ounces) tomatoes

Kosher salt and pepper to taste

1 teaspoon paprika

2 pounds raw shrimp

1-1/2 teaspoons gumbo filé

1/4 to 1/2 teaspoon Tabasco sauce

1. Melt the butter in a large skillet or heavy saucepan. Stir in the onions, garlic, and green peppers; cook over a low heat until they are tender, stirring frequently.

2. Pour in the tomatoes and simmer for 25 to 30 minutes. Season with salt, pepper, and paprika. While tomato mixture is cooking, remove the shells from the shrimp and clean them. Add to the sauce and continue to cook for 5 minutes more.

3. Stir in gumbo filé and Tabasco sauce. Serve immediately over popcorn rice.

Popcorn Rice or White Rice

2 cups uncooked rice (popcorn or white)

4 cups water

2 tablespoons unsalted butter

2 teaspoons kosher salt

1. Combine ingredients in a 2- or 3-quart saucepan.

2. Bring to a boil and stir once or twice; lower heat.

3. Cover tightly and simmer for 15 minutes, or until rice is tender and all the liquid is absorbed.

4. Fluff with fork and serve. (For drier rice, use 1/4 cup less water.)

NOTE: Popcorn rice is available from:

Stansel Rice Company
Gueydan, Louisiana
(337) 536–6140 phone
(337) 536–6143 fax
riceman@stanselrice.com

Sugar Snap Peas and Baby Yellow Pattypan Squash with Chives

Pattypan squash (cymling) is a round flat squash with a scalloped edge. For a good flavor, the inside of the squash should be slightly green in color, not white. Quick cooking is always the key with fresh vegetables, ensuring both a crisp texture and a bright color.

3/4 pound sugar snap peas

3 tablespoons unsalted butter

3/4 pound pattypan squash, cut into 2-inch pieces

Kosher salt and freshly ground black pepper

Chopped fresh parsley and chives

1 teaspoon roasted or minced garlic (optional)

1. Blanch sugar snap peas for 1 minute in boiling salted water. Immediately plunge sugar snaps into cool running water. Once cool, drain and set aside.

2. Heat butter in a skillet over moderate heat. Add pattypan squash; sauté, shaking the pan occasionally, for about 2 minutes.

3. Add sugar snap peas and remaining ingredients; cook only until vegetables are very hot. Serve immediately.

Buttermilk Biscuits

2 cups all-purpose flour

1 tablespoon baking powder

1/2 teaspoon kosher salt

4 tablespoons unsalted butter

3/4 cup buttermilk

1. Sift together flour, baking powder, and salt.

2. Cut the butter with two knives until the mixture is the consistency of coarse cornmeal. (This can also be achieved by using a food processor.) Add to flour mixture.

3. Stir in the buttermilk and make a soft dough. Knead on a lightly floured board for approximately one minute.

4. Roll out the dough to about 1/2 inch thick, adding more flour to the board if necessary.

5. Cut into 2-inch rounds with a floured biscuit cutter.

6. Bake on an ungreased baking sheet at 450 degrees for about 12 minutes or until the biscuits are browned.

Black Walnut Cake

4 large eggs, separated

1 cup zwieback crumbs

1 cup black walnuts, finely chopped

2/3 cup powdered sugar

1 teaspoon vanilla extract

1/2 cup heavy cream, whipped

1. Beat the egg yolks lightly.

2. Mix the zwieback crumbs with chopped nuts, egg yolks, sugar, and vanilla.

3. Beat the egg whites until stiff; gently fold into mixture and pile into a buttered shallow casserole dish.

4. Bake in a 350-degree oven, 20 to 25 minutes. If possible, let stand overnight before serving.

NOTE: Black walnuts are available from some specialty food stores, including:

American Spoon Foods, Inc.
P.O. Box 566
Petoskey, Michigan 49770-0566
www.spoon.com

SPRING BRUNCH

ADVANCE PREPARATION NOTES

1 DAY BEFORE THE BRUNCH

Make granita (can be done up to one week before).

Clean and dry lettuce.

Dice bacon.

Make vinaigrette for salad.

Buy or bake cookies.

DAY OF THE BRUNCH

Make Salmon Soufflé.

Make Herbed Toast Triangles.

Cook bacon while soufflé is baking.

Finish wilted salad when soufflé is ready.

Prepare fruit garnish for granita, if using. Chill well.

Easy, light, and unusual, Salmon Soufflé was one of Russel's favorite foods for spring entertaining. He would have liked the combination of colors in this meal, the pale-coral soufflé with the spring green of the salad and the magenta strawberry granita, as well as its celebration of seasonality; at Dragon Rock, the food, like the décor, changed with the seasons.

MENU (serves 6)

Salmon Soufflé

Wilted Salad with Bacon

Herbed Toast Triangles

Strawberry Granita with Little Cookies

Salmon Soufflé

For maximum effect, rush the soufflé to the table as soon as it comes out of the oven. Exclaim "Voila!" to your guests if you want to. But you needn't stress out about it—the soufflé can wait 5 minutes or so to be served; it will have fallen a bit but will taste just as good.

Unsalted butter for greasing the pan

Fine dry bread crumbs

3 tablespoons unsalted butter

4 tablespoons flour

1-1/2 teaspoons curry powder
(we like Sun Brand or Javin)

1-1/2 cups milk, warmed with 1 small sprig fresh thyme

1-1/2 teaspoons kosher salt

Freshly ground black pepper to taste

A few gratings of fresh nutmeg

6 large egg yolks

1-1/2 cups cooked fresh salmon filet (3/4-pound
skinless center-cut filet) or use canned salmon,
picked-over

7 large egg whites

Fresh lemon juice for serving

Coarse sea salt for serving

Finely chopped scallion for serving

1. Preheat the oven to 400 degrees. Generously coat the bottom and sides of a 2-1/2- to 3-quart soufflé or straight-sided baking dish with butter and then bread crumbs. This will help the soufflé rise up the sides of the dish more easily. Set the baking dish on a baking sheet lined with parchment, foil, or a sheet of Silpat.

2. Heat the butter in a large heavy-bottomed saucepan; when it is foaming, add the flour and curry powder. Cook for 3 minutes on low heat, stirring. This is called a roux.

3. Remove the thyme sprig from the milk; add the warm milk, salt, pepper, and nutmeg to the roux, whisking to prevent lumps. Cook over low heat, stirring, until the sauce thickens and starts to bubble.

4. Remove the pan from the heat; add the egg yolks one at a time, beating well after each addition until the sauce is thoroughly blended. Stir in the salmon.

5. Beat the whites to stiff, but not dry, peaks with a pinch of salt. Take about a quarter of the whites and stir into the soufflé base. Gently fold in the remaining whites until only a few puffs of white remain. Scrape the mixture into the prepared baking dish.

6. Put the soufflé in the oven on the lowest rack and immediately reduce the heat to 375 degrees. Bake until a toothpick inserted in the center comes out clean, about 25 to 30 minutes.

7. Serve immediately, adding a squirt of lemon juice and a light sprinkling of sea salt and scallion to each portion.

Wilted Salad with Bacon

The sweet tenderness of Boston lettuce is a perfect match for the salmon, but for another meal, try this salad with young dandelion greens, frisée, or curly endive.

3 tablespoons red wine vinegar

2 tablespoons Dijon mustard

Kosher salt and freshly ground black pepper
    to taste

3 tablespoons grapeseed or peanut oil

6 cups washed, dried, and torn Boston lettuce

6 ounces slab bacon

1/2 cup walnuts

1. Whisk the vinegar and mustard with the salt and pepper. Whisk in the oil until emulsified. Set aside. Put the lettuce into a serving bowl.

2. Cut the bacon into 1/4-inch dice and cook slowly in a skillet. When it is almost crisp, add the walnuts, and cook until crisp.

3. Add the vinaigrette to the skillet, stirring; let it bubble for a minute, then pour over the lettuce. Add salt and pepper to taste and serve immediately.

Herbed Toast Triangles

2 tablespoons unsalted butter

1 teaspoon finely chopped flat-leaf parsley

Kosher salt and freshly ground black pepper to taste

6 slices thin-sliced white sandwich bread, crusts removed, cut into 2 triangles each

1. Melt the butter in a small saucepan with the parsley, salt, and pepper.

2. Brush the bread on both sides with the herb butter.

3. Bake at 350 degrees until golden, about 10 minutes, turning once halfway through baking.

Strawberry Granita with Little Cookies

Granitas are amazingly easy to make, and the technique is easily adapted to many different kinds of fruit. Some of our favorites are watermelon, pineapple, blood orange, grapefruit, and raspberry. Fresh-brewed espresso sweetened with sugar makes a wonderful granita and is especially good garnished with whipped cream. Granitas stay fresh for up to a week.

1 pint strawberries, hulled and cut in half

1/4 cup sugar

1 teaspoon fresh lemon juice

Dash of kosher salt

2 tablespoons late-harvest Riesling dessert wine

Blueberries, raspberries, blackberries, little melon balls, or pineapple dice for garnish, if desired

1. Put all the granita ingredients in the work bowl of a food processor or blender and process until a smooth purée is achieved.

2. Transfer to a 2-quart (or larger) container; put in the freezer for 1 hour, or until it starts to freeze. Break up the hardened parts with a fork or a whisk, then return to the freezer. Continue this process of breaking up the frozen parts every 30 to 45 minutes or so (depending on how well your freezer works) until you end up with a kind of frozen slush. (This is a great project for kids.) Cover.

3. Serve in chilled bowls with one of the above garnishes if desired. Accompany with store-bought butter cookies and tiny glasses of well-chilled dessert wine.

SUNDAY SUPPER

ADVANCE PREPARATION NOTES

DAY BEFORE THE SUPPER

Make Gingerbread, cool, wrap well. Reheat before serving.

Clean and cut portobellos and scallions.

In a perfect world, Sunday supper can be a pleasant, calm time to savor the last hours of the weekend with friends or family before the work- or school-week begins. In our house, it tended to be a bit hectic, with Russel and me spending much of our time getting ready to leave Dragon Rock, our weekend home, to return to Manhattan. Our two cats, Juneberg and Sugar, much preferred country life (and its attendant wildlife) and were quite adept at finding hiding places to keep from having to go back to the city. Somehow, they knew that Sunday night meant the end of their country weekend, too.

MENU (serves 8)

Chicken Baked in Cream on a Bed of Watercress

Roasted Portobello Mushrooms and Scallions

Buttered Egg Noodles

Warm Gingerbread

Chicken Baked in Cream on a Bed of Watercress

Cooking the chicken in cream keeps it moist and gives it a silky texture. Cutting it up in the manner described below, with the breast halves larger than the dark-meat portions, ensures that the dark and white meat will be done at the same time. We like to start with the best chickens: kosher (the Empire brand is widely available in supermarkets across the country) or Eberly (also sold under the D'Artagnan label), a free-range brand. Not all free-range or "natural" chickens are equally good; some tend to be dry or have an odd texture, so if you can't find the brands mentioned above, keep trying those available in your area until you find one you like.

2 (3 to 3-1/2-pound) chickens, kosher or free-range, each cut into 8 pieces (2 breast halves, 2 wings, 2 drumsticks, 2 thighs)

Kosher salt and freshly ground black pepper

2 tablespoons unsalted butter

1 tablespoon canola, safflower, or vegetable oil

1/2 cup Fino or other dry sherry

2 teaspoons finely chopped garlic

2 teaspoons chopped fresh thyme leaves

2 cups heavy cream

2 bunches watercress, trimmed to 1 inch below the leaves

1. Rinse the chicken well under cold water, pat dry with paper towels, and season with salt and pepper.

2. Heat the butter and oil in a large (12 inches or so) heavy-bottomed skillet. When the butter starts to brown, add the chicken pieces, skin-side-down, in a single layer without crowding; cook over medium-high heat, turning, until browned on all sides. (To avoid crowding, fry in several batches.) If you try to turn a piece and it seems to be sticking to the pan, leave it alone for a few minutes. When it is properly browned and ready to be turned, it will have formed a crust on the bottom that will help the chicken release from the pan (this makes many people nervous, but it really works). As the chicken browns, put the pieces into a shallow baking dish (a lasagna pan works well) that just fits them in a single layer set on a sheet pan.

3. Pour off the fat from the pan, return to the stove, and add the sherry. Cook over medium-high heat, scraping the brown bits from the bottom, until the sherry reduces slightly. Add the garlic, thyme, and cream; season sparingly with salt and pepper (the sauce will reduce when baked and become too salty if you're not careful). When the liquid comes to a simmer, pour into the baking dish with the chicken, turning the chicken to coat. Leave the chicken skin-side-down.

4. Cover the baking dish tightly and bake in a preheated 350-degree oven. After 20 minutes, turn the chicken skin-side-up and cook for 10 minutes more. Uncover and bake until the sauce has thickened slightly and has a nut-brown cast, about 10 minutes more. Adjust the seasoning if necessary.

5. Line 8 plates or a serving platter with the watercress, arrange the chicken on it, and pour the sauce over.

Roasted Portobello Mushrooms and Scallions

2-1/2 pounds portobello mushrooms

12 scallions

1/2 cup fruity olive oil

Kosher salt and freshly ground black pepper to taste

2 tablespoons chopped flat-leaf parsley

1 teaspoon minced garlic

1. Discard the portobello stems, wipe the caps clean with a damp paper towel, and cut into wedges about 1 inch at the widest point.

2. Rinse the scallions, cut off the root end, and cut the white and light green parts into 1-inch pieces. Toss with the mushrooms, oil, salt, and pepper; roast in a single layer in a preheated 450-degree oven until the mushrooms are tender and the scallions are browned, about 20 minutes. When almost done, add the parsley and garlic.

Gingerbread

1-1/2 cups flour

1 tablespoon cocoa powder

1/2 teaspoon baking soda

1-1/2 teaspoons baking powder

1/4 teaspoon kosher salt

2 teaspoons ground ginger

1 teaspoon cinnamon

1/4 teaspoon ground cloves

1/4 pound unsalted butter at room temperature

1/4 cup sugar

1/2 cup dark brown sugar

1/2 cup sour cream

1/2 cup molasses

2 large eggs

2 tablespoons finely grated, peeled fresh gingerroot

Confectioners' sugar, to serve

1. Sift the flour, cocoa, baking soda, baking powder, salt, and spices together.

2. Cream the butter until it lightens in texture and color. Add the sugars; cream until fluffy. Add the sour cream and molasses; beat well. Add eggs one at a time; blend well, then stir in the fresh ginger and dry ingredients until combined. Scrape into a buttered 9-inch-square baking pan.

3. Bake in a preheated 350-degree oven until a toothpick inserted in the center comes out clean, 25 to 30 minutes. Let cool for about 10 minutes, then cut into squares and sprinkle with confectioners' sugar.

COMFORT FOOD DINNER

ADVANCE PREPARATION NOTES

1 DAY BEFORE THE DINNER

Make gelatin.

Make Veal Stew through Step 4 (can do up to 3 days before).

Make Spaetzle.

Toast hazelnuts.

DAY OF THE DINNER

Complete Step 1 of Brussels Sprouts recipe early in the day; finish recipe while reheating stew.

Clean, trim, cut, and chill lettuce; make the dressing. Chill salad plates if space permits.

Degrease and reheat veal stew.

Chop parsley.

Make sour cream–paprika garnish.

About 5 minutes before the stew is ready, reheat Spaetzle in a skillet with butter, salt, and pepper.

Unmold gelatin onto a serving platter before guests arrive; cover loosely with plastic wrap.

Keep refrigerated until serving time.

Russel loved this veal stew, especially with the addition of sour cream, and it was crucial that the paprika be sprinkled on top of the sour cream just so. He also loved the deep colors of the veal and its sauce on chutney brown American Modern, and I think he would have felt the same way about our addition of roasted Brussels Sprouts with Toasted Hazelnuts. It is a rich, hearty, and masculine meal, which may be why he liked it so much.

MENU (serves 6)

Hungarian Veal Stew

Brussels Sprouts with Toasted Hazelnuts

Spaetzle

Iceberg Lettuce Wedges with Vinegar-Cream Dressing

Pink Grapefruit Gelatin

Hungarian Veal Stew

3 tablespoons lard

1-1/2 cups finely chopped onion

Kosher salt and freshly ground
black pepper to taste

2 teaspoons minced garlic

3 pounds boneless veal shoulder,
trimmed of sinew and cut into
1-inch cubes

3 tablespoons sweet Hungarian
paprika, plus additional for garnish

Dash of cayenne pepper

Wondra flour for coating veal

3/4 cup tomato purée

1-1/2 teaspoons tomato paste

1-1/2 cups chicken stock

3/4 teaspoon caraway seed

2 tablespoons chopped flat-leaf
parsley

6 tablespoons sour cream, plus
additional for garnish

1. Heat the lard in a heavy-bottomed Dutch oven. Add the onion, salt, and pepper; cook over medium-low heat until tender and translucent. Add the garlic; cook for a few seconds longer, just until you start to smell the garlic. Remove the onion-garlic mixture with a slotted spoon, leaving the fat in the pan. Reserve.

2. Season the veal with salt, pepper, paprika, and cayenne pepper; toss with enough flour to lightly coat it.

3. Raise the heat to medium and add the veal in a single layer, allowing space around each piece so the veal sears rather than steams (do this in several batches). Cook until the veal develops a golden crust. As each batch is done, put the pieces in the upside-down lid of the Dutch oven or on a platter to collect the juices that accumulate. If the bottom of the pan starts to look dry, add a little more lard.

4. Return the cooked onion to the pan; add the tomato purée, tomato paste, chicken stock, and caraway seed. Bring to a simmer, cover, and cook over low heat (to maintain a bare simmer) until the veal is tender (the point of a small knife should go through with no resistance), about 1-1/2 to 2 hours. The stew may be prepared up to 2 days ahead at this point, then slowly reheated, covered, until you are ready to proceed with the rest of the recipe.

5. Stir in the parsley and sour cream; heat to warm through, being careful not to let it boil. Garnish with a spoonful of sour cream made pink with a little paprika.

Stew Tips

The best and neatest way to season and flour the veal is on a sheet pan lined with wax paper, which can be discarded when used, leaving a clean pan.

Stainless-steel spring-loaded tongs are perfect for turning the pieces of veal. They cost very little and are essential cook's tools.

Don't be appalled at our use of lard here: it is lower in saturated fat than butter and gives this stew just the right flavor and texture.

Brussels Sprouts with Toasted Hazelnuts

1-1/2 pounds brussels sprouts, trimmed and cut into halves lengthwise

5 tablespoons unsalted butter, melted

3/4 teaspoons chopped fresh thyme

Kosher salt and freshly ground black pepper

1/4 cup coarsely chopped, toasted blanched hazelnuts

Hazelnut oil to taste

1. Cook the brussels sprouts in boiling salted water until half-tender, about 3 minutes. Drain, then toss with the butter, thyme, salt, and pepper. Put into a shallow baking dish or sheet pan lined with parchment.

2. Bake at 450 degrees for 20 minutes, until browned and tender. Add hazelnuts and drizzle with hazelnut oil just before serving.

Spaetzle

Spaetzle are easy, though a bit messy, to make and can be served plain, as they are here, or sautéed in butter with homemade dry bread crumbs and fresh chives, parsley, or dill. They are also delicious when baked with heavy cream and Parmesan. We like to make them a day or two ahead to avoid last-minute mess and stress while entertaining. If you're pressed for time, noodles make a good substitute in this meal.

2/3 cup milk

4 large eggs, plus 2 yolks

1 teaspoon kosher salt

1/8 teaspoon freshly ground black pepper

2-1/4 cups flour

3 to 4 tablespoons unsalted butter, softened, for serving

1. Whisk together the milk, eggs, yolks, salt, and pepper. Sift the flour over the wet ingredients and whisk to blend. Cover and let rest for an hour or so.

2. Bring a large pot of salted water to a boil. With a rubber spatula, push the spaetzle batter through the holes of a slotted spoon into the boiling water (any other implement with similar-sized holes can be used; or use a spaetzle-maker, which is quite inexpensive). Work in batches so you don't crowd the pot. (Spraying the spoon with nonstick cooking spray helps speed up the process a bit.) Spaetzle are done 1 minute after they come to the surface.

3. To serve right away, simply drain in a colander and toss with butter, salt, and pepper. If serving at another time, put the spaetzle into a bowl of ice water to stop the cooking, then drain. Toss with canola or safflower oil; cover and refrigerate for up to 2 days.

Iceberg Lettuce Wedges with Vinegar-Cream Dressing

1 large head iceberg lettuce

6 tablespoons sugar

6 tablespoons rice wine vinegar

9 tablespoons heavy cream

Dash of kosher salt, freshly ground black pepper

3 scallions, white and light green parts only, sliced thin

1. Cut the core off the bottom of the lettuce head. Remove any loose or discolored outer leaves; cut the lettuce into 8 wedges. Rinse, dry, and chill.
2. With a whisk, combine the remaining ingredients and let sit for a few minutes to allow the sugar to dissolve.
3. Serve the lettuce on chilled plates with the dressing spooned over the wedges.

Pink Grapefruit Gelatin

If you don't feel like squeezing your own grapefruit juice, you can buy it. Be sure to get the real thing, not the pasteurized kind. Also, you can vary this recipe by using other fruits like blood oranges, tangerines, or Meyer lemons. Just adjust the sugar according to how tart the fruit is.

1 or 2 pink grapefruits for sectioning

4 cups freshly squeezed pink grapefruit juice

6 envelopes unflavored gelatin

1 cup sugar

1-1/2 cups water

Optional garnish: mint, lemon verbena, or long
   strips of grapefruit zest

1. With a sharp knife or a bread knife, cut the bottom or top ends off the grapefruit so it can lie flat. Remove the skin and white pith by cutting down the grapefruit from top to bottom, working your way around and trying to keep the round shape of the grapefruit as you go. Holding the fruit in your hand or on a cutting board, cut out the sections by inserting the knife next to the side of each membrane and cutting down. Set grapefruit sections aside.

2. Pour 1 cup of the grapefruit juice into a mixing bowl. Sprinkle the unflavored gelatin over the juice and allow gelatin to soften for around five minutes.

3. Over medium-high heat, bring the sugar and water to a boil, stirring occasionally in order to dissolve the sugar. Pour this mixture over the gelatin/juice mixture; with a wire whisk or spoon, stir all ingredients well to completely dissolve the gelatin. Add the remaining three cups of grapefruit juice.

4. Pour into a terrine or loaf pan (sprayed with oil or lined with plastic wrap if you wish to unmold for serving). Place in refrigerator until set, approximately 4 hours. After about 45 minutes or when gelatin has begun to set, place the grapefruit sections in the terrine or loaf pan. Cover with plastic wrap until ready to serve.

5. To serve, cut in slices, or unmold it by wrapping a hot wet cloth around the bottom and sides of the pan. Run a butter knife around the edge, put a platter over the top, and turn upside down. If it doesn't come out easily, try the hot cloth again.

6. Garnish with mint, lemon verbena, or grapefruit zest.

GREEN AND WHITE COCKTAIL PARTY

ADVANCE PREPARATION NOTES

1 DAY BEFORE THE PARTY

Trim vegetables for Crudités.

Cook Quail Eggs.

Make Tarragon Mayonnaise, Watercress Dip, Céleri Rémoulade.

Cut and crisp Celery Boats.

DAY OF THE PARTY

Cut and blanch Crudités (set them up in a basket or on a platter hours ahead of time). Wrap well and refrigerate.

Whenever you'd like, put the Wasabi Peas, White Anchovies, Spiced Pepitas, and Granny Smith apples in bowls; set out in various spots in the room where your party will be held.

Up to 2 hours before serving, cook the Potatoes but do not refrigerate. Top with sour cream and dill a few minutes before serving.

Up to 2 hours before serving, cut and garnish Quail Eggs. Refrigerate, loosely covered, in a single layer (on the serving platter if you have the space).

Make Onion Sandwiches several hours ahead, if you'd like. Cover with damp paper towels and plastic wrap; refrigerate until half an hour before serving.

2 hours before serving, make the cheese platter; cover with plastic wrap and leave out at room temperature.

Up to 1 hour before serving, slice French bread for cheese and put in a plastic bag.

Up to 1 hour before serving, finish the Celery Boats.

When guests arrive, cook Edamame and toss with coarse sea salt.

While looking through Russel's original menu cookbook, we found a page titled "Appetizer Suggestions for December 26th." It included instructions for the housekeeper to go to Colette Pastry Shop to purchase quiche, and also had a heading called "Other Suggestions," which listed "white" foods (such as canned quail eggs, fennel, and pickled cauliflower) and "other colors." Annie had no memory of this party (perhaps it was before she was born, or was an idea that was never realized). Deciding to take the general concept and run with it, we came up with this menu.

MENU (serves 12)

Green and White Crudités with Herbed Watercress Dip

Sweet Onion Sandwiches with Chopped Parsley Rims

Peeled Little Potatoes with Sour Cream and Dill

Celery Boats with Robiola Osella and White Truffle Oil

Céleri Rémoulade on Apple Slices

Platter of White Cheeses with Green Grapes

Hard-cooked Quail Eggs with Tarragon Mayonnaise and Asparagus Tips

Bowls of Edamame with Sea Salt, Wasabi Peas, White Anchovy Fillets, Granny Smith Apples, and Spiced Pepitas

Green and White Crudités with Herbed Watercress Dip

Use any combination of the following:

Haricots vert or green beans

Fennel

Baby white asparagus

Baby zucchini or green pattypan squash

Endive

Jicama

1. Buy about 2 pounds total of the vegetables that you choose; more, depending on the size of your platter or container. Your guests may not eat all the crudités, but the display should look beautiful and bountiful.

2. Cut the beans at the stem end only, then blanch and chill.

3. Trim the fennel so that just the bottom bulbs remain and remove any outer layers that are tough, stringy, or discolored. Then cut the fennel bulbs into thin wedges.

4. Leave baby white asparagus, baby zucchini, or green pattypans whole; blanch and chill.

5. Cut the endive into spears.

6. Peel the jicama with a chef's knife (more efficient than a peeler for this); cut into batons (like celery sticks).

Vegetable Tip

To keep the blanched vegetables from becoming watery as they chill, wrap them in layers of paper towels before putting in plastic bags.

Herbed Watercress Dip

2 small bunches watercress, portions below leaves discarded

1-1/2 cups mayonnaise

4 teaspoons fresh lemon juice

2 teaspoons chopped fresh dill

1 teaspoon chopped chives

4 tablespoons sour cream

Kosher salt and freshly ground black pepper to taste

Process the watercress in a food processor or blender until chopped; add the remaining ingredients and process until blended, allowing some flecks of green to remain.

Dip Tip

Herbed Watercress Dip also makes a tasty and easy sauce for fish or chicken.

Sweet Onion Sandwiches with Chopped Parsley Rims

1 medium white or Spanish onion

Mayonnaise

Kosher salt and freshly ground black pepper

About 1-1/2 cups finely chopped flat-leaf parsley

24 slices (one bag) Pepperidge Farm Very Thin White Bread

Chives for garnish

1. Peel the onion, cut off the stem and root ends, and cut in half lengthwise. For no-tears onion-slicing, let the peeled and cut onion sit for about 5 minutes in cold water to cover; then slice the onion thinly. To achieve sweet-tasting onion slices, soak them again in fresh cold water for another 5 minutes.

2. For each sandwich, spread mayonnaise on two pieces of bread, top one with a thin layer of onion, salt, and pepper. Press lightly, top with the second piece of bread, and then trim off the crust. (Make the sandwiches assembly line–style on a large cutting board or work surface. Use a 2-inch round cutter and cut 3 rounds per sandwich. Roll the edges in mayonnaise, then in parsley. Cover with damp paper towels and plastic wrap; refrigerate. Serve on a bed of chives.

Peeled Little Potatoes with Sour Cream and Dill

12 tiny potatoes, preferably Yukon Golds
(or use any evenly shaped small potato)

1/2 cup sour cream

Fresh dill sprigs

Coarse sea salt and freshly ground black pepper to taste

1. Peel the potatoes and put them in cold water to prevent discoloration. Cut each one in half to make ovals or rounds, whichever looks better. Cut off a little piece from each bottom to stabilize. With a melon baller, make a small hollow in the top side. Put in a pot of cold salted water.

2. Bring the water to a simmer; cover and cook until potatoes are tender when tested with a paring knife. Drain in a colander under cold running water.

3. Top with sour cream, dill sprigs, sea salt, and pepper. Serve on a bed of dill sprigs.

Celery Boats with Robiola Osella and White Truffle Oil

2 or 3 celery stalks

Robiola Osella
(a soft, mild, cream cheese–like Italian cheese;
Saint André makes a decent substitute)

White truffle oil

Kosher salt and freshly ground pepper to taste

Celery leaves for garnish

1. Peel the celery and cut 2-inch diagonal pieces. Store in the refrigerator in a jar of cold water to crisp.

2. Dry the celery well and place on a platter. Put the Robiola on top as little dots or as a ribbon, drizzle with truffle oil (use sparingly; it's quite strong), and season with salt and pepper. Garnish the platter with celery leaves.

Céleri Rémoulade on Apple Slices

1/4 cup mayonnaise

2 teaspoons fresh lemon juice

1/2 teaspoon grained mustard

3/4 teaspoon Dijon mustard

1 teaspoon finely chopped flat-leaf parsley

1 teaspoon sour cream

Kosher salt and freshly ground black pepper to taste

Peeled celery root cut into matchsticks (about 2 cups)

1 Granny Smith apple

Fresh bay leaves for garnish

1. To make the rémoulade sauce, whisk together the mayonnaise, lemon juice, mustards, parsley, sour cream, salt, and pepper. Toss with the celery root.

2. Shortly before serving, trim the ends of the apple, quarter, and cut out the core, then cut into 1/4-inch slices (1 Granny Smith should yield about 30 slices). Sprinkle with lemon juice after cutting to prevent discoloration.

3. Put little haystacks of the céleri rémoulade on top of each slice. Garnish the platter with fresh bay leaves.

Platter of White Cheeses with Green Grapes

2 to 3 pounds of 3 white cheeses of different shapes and flavors.

> **Suggestions:**
>
> **Brillat-Savarin**
>
> **Caciotta Siena**
>
> **Explorateur**
>
> **Feta**
>
> **Goat logs, pyramids, or buttons**
>
> **Mozzarella**
>
> **Pecorino Sardo**
>
> **Ricotta salata**
>
> **Stracchino**

Green grapes (and fresh green figs, if desired)

French bread, sliced

Fig, grape, lemon, fresh bay, or galax leaves or thyme sprigs for garnish.

1. Remove cheese from the refrigerator 2 hours before serving.

2. Leave the cheeses whole for the most attractive presentation. Garnish the platter with fresh fig, grape, lemon, fresh bay, or galax leaves or fresh thyme sprigs. Keep it simple, sculptural, and unfussy. Fill in the spaces between the cheeses with green grapes and/or fresh green figs. Serve with French bread. (No crackers.)

Hard-Cooked Quail Eggs with Tarragon Mayonnaise and Asparagus Tips

Quail eggs are available at good butcher shops, poultry farms, and Japanese and Chinese markets. They look lovely on a bed of alfalfa sprouts or mâche. Chicken eggs can be substituted, but they won't look as sweet.

1 dozen quail eggs

Pot of salted water

24 fresh asparagus tips

Tarragon Mayonnaise

2 tablespoons mayonnaise

1/2 teaspoon chopped tarragon

1/4 teaspoon fresh lemon juice

1/4 teaspoon Dijon mustard

Kosher salt and freshly ground black pepper to taste

Alfalfa sprouts or mâche to garnish the platter

1. Put the quail eggs in a small pot, cover with cold water and bring to a boil. Turn off the heat; cover and let sit for 3 minutes. Plunge into cold water, then peel. Cover and chill.

2. Bring a pot of salted water to boil, add the asparagus tips, and cook until crisp and tender. Plunge into cold water, then dry and chill.

3. Whisk together the mayonnaise, tarragon, lemon juice, mustard, salt, and pepper.

4. To serve, halve the quail eggs, top with a dab of the tarragon mayonnaise and then an asparagus tip. Season with salt and pepper.

Tips for Easier Entertaining

Planning and Organizing

When planning a menu, choose dishes that can be made ahead, things that won't suffer if dinner is delayed, and items that taste good at room temperature. Select a menu that is appropriate to the season, the occasion, and the tastes of your guests. Have a variety of flavors and textures in the meal, and if you're having a rich entrée, serve a refreshing light dessert. When planning a cocktail party where you will be serving hors d'oeuvres, serve 6 to 8 different kinds and figure on a total of about 12 pieces per person for a two-hour party. If you think the party may last longer or know your guests are hearty eaters, increase the quantities. Choose a mixture of hot and cold foods, with a selection of vegetable, fish, meat, and cheese-based items. Items to be warmed can be set up on parchment-lined baking sheets, ready to go in the oven when needed. Platters and trays can be set up in advance with garnishes and cold food, if refrigerator space permits.

While picking out instant party foods in Chinatown, Japantown, Little India, or the like, buy garnishes such as fresh curry leaves, dried banana leaves, Chinese long beans, and flowering chives. Inexpensive place mats, bowls, trays, fabrics, and such are also available to decorate the table and set a mood.

Make a shopping list that is organized by store and by aisle. Buy wine and nonperishables ahead of time.

Store prepped ingredients in stackable plastic containers with lids or zip-top bags. They stay fresher and take up less room in the refrigerator than bowls.

Clean pots, cutting boards, utensils, etc., as you go, both before and during the party.

Have plenty of ice, about 1 pound per person. To save time, effort, and money, have it delivered by a local ice company rather than buying it at the supermarket. Order it in plastic containers, which take up less space and won't leak all over your floor like the bags do.

Leave extra time for mishaps or things forgotten.

Have clean plates, glasses, and table linens counted out and ready to go. Set the table the night before, if feasible. Figure on 2 to 3 glasses per person, especially for big parties.

Set up an area to "land" baking pans, casseroles, etc., as they come out of the oven. The top of the stove, if it's free, is a good place, as is a cooling rack set on the counter or a table.

If you're serving buffet-style and there is enough space in the refrigerator or on the counter, have back-up platters set up with food ahead of time to replace those that run low on the buffet.

To avoid having guests peer over your shoulder in the kitchen, have a separate bar/snack area set up with glasses, mixers, ice, bar fruit, drinks, and napkins. Have music playing and an amusing guest to keep the others entertained while you finish up in the kitchen.

Consider structuring one of the menus in this book as a potluck. Give each person a recipe. Use your serving pieces, not theirs, to maintain a unified look.

Pantry and Freezer Items

Truffle butter and truffle oil, aged balsamic vinegar, nut oils, flavored oils, and the great variety of domestic and imported sea salts are all great flavor and texture boosters when added to simply prepared foods just before serving. Try white truffle oil on sliced mozzarella, and over sautéed or roasted mushrooms or chicken; aged balsamic with fresh strawberries, or on a chunk of Parmigiano-Reggiano; nut oils or flavored oils in salads; coarse sea salt over mashed potatoes, eggs any style, buttered French bread, or grilled fish.

Frozen puff pastry and phyllo are wonderful for quick hors d'oeuvres. For example, you can cut small rounds of puff pastry, top them with chopped anchovies, grated Gruyere, a slice of cherry tomato with chopped basil, or any number of things, and bake until browned. Or buy a cooked kielbasa or similar sausage, roll out the puff pastry to form a rectangle, roll the sausage up in it with mustard, brush with cream and bake until golden. It looks impressive and tastes great, but it's really just a gussied-up pig-in-a-blanket. Use store-bought red pepper spread, fresh basil, or marjoram and soft goat cheese to make a savory strudel with phyllo (see p. 91 for instructions on filling and rolling). These are just suggestions; feel free to improvise with what you like and what you have on hand.

Veal or duck demi-glace (the D'Artagnan brand is particularly good), available frozen, is the perfect base for a sauce for meat or poultry. Simply reduce red wine until syrupy, add the demi-glace and fresh herbs appropriate to the dish, simmer for 10 minutes, then add a couple of tablespoons of butter.

Handkerchief bread or lahvash (sold in plastic bags in gourmet, health-food, and Middle Eastern food stores) and flour and corn tortillas are great to keep in the freezer for making quesadillas and piadinas (the Italian version of a quesadilla). The tortillas can be filled with grated cheese (Jack, Muenster, Cotija, among others) and sautéed chorizo or chard, mushrooms, cooked corn, and zucchini, then folded over and sautéed till crisp. (See any good Mexican or Southwestern cookbook for more filling suggestions.) Lahvash can be used similarly, but with more Mediterranean fillings such as Mozzarella and Prosciutto or sautéed greens; Ricotta salata; or Feta with roasted eggplant or roasted tomatoes. Cut in small wedges and serve warm (they can be sautéed in advance and then reheated in the oven and cut before serving).

Instant Hors D'oeuvres from the Pantry and Deli

Try these variations to brighten any party:

Spanish, Italian, or Portuguese tuna in olive oil, roasted peppers, and olives with bread sticks and slices of French or Italian bread.

Roasted red pepper spread, olivada, or tapenade with crumbled soft goat cheese on store-bought toasts.

White bean purée made in the food processor with canned white beans (such as cannellini), parsley, lemon juice, garlic and fruity olive oil, served with homemade or store-bought toasts.

Smoked salmon with buttered cocktail pumpernickel, lemon, and capers (a good American or Scottish brand packed in cryovac can be kept in the freezer for emergencies).

Spiced nuts, wasabi peas, and cheese sticks.

Prosciutto or Italian salami with melon or figs and cracked black pepper.

>LIST CONTINUED>

Crudités made with precut vegetables (or those that need little or no cutting) from the supermarket with fruity olive oil and coarse sea salt as a dip. For a more stylish presentation, avoid the every-color-in-the-rainbow look and choose vegetables in just two or three colors (see p. 125 for ideas). Food stores in ethnic neighborhoods are great sources for party food, both fresh and frozen.

Chinese butcher shops: frozen wontons and dumplings made in-house using good ingredients.

Japanese markets: frozen dumplings and crispy cocktail snacks, including wasabi peas and seaweed crackers (the Japanese equivalent of potato chips).

Greek and Middle Eastern stores: delicious flatbreads, olives, and homemade dips (such as taramosalata, hummus, and baba ghanouj).

Polish butcher shops: kielbasa—to sauté, cut up and serve with small pieces of rye bread—and Polish mustard.

Indian markets: chutneys, raitas, breads, and all sorts of condiments.

A variety of salad combinations serve to whet and satisfy the appetite:

Arugula with sliced pears, toasted almonds, and shaved Parmesan.

Frisée with roasted beets, walnuts, and Roquefort.

Mâche with smoked salmon or trout, sliced cucumbers, and scallions.

Sliced summer tomatoes with olives (such as Kalamata or Niçoise), crumbled goat cheese, fruity olive oil, fresh basil or mint, and a squirt of lemon juice.

Arugula with fresh figs, caciotta (or any young sheep- or goat-milk cheese), and toasted pine nuts.

Sweet chili sauce, with a little lime juice and grated ginger added, makes a fast and tasty way to cook chicken: just pour over chicken parts and bake at 400 degrees till done.

Thai curry paste, available in tins and plastic bags (look for brands with all natural ingredients), is a great timesaver: put some in a skillet, add canned coconut milk, keffir lime leaves (or lime juice), and some brown sugar; cook till slightly thickened. Add cooked chicken, pork, seafood, or duck (from the Chinese takeout), warm through, and serve over rice garnished with chopped cilantro.

Ketjap manis, also known as sweet soy sauce, is an Indonesian condiment that makes a perfect glaze for roasted meats and poultry. Thin it down a little with some soy sauce, and add more flavor with Asian sesame oil and grated ginger. Brush on the glaze when the meat has about 15 minutes of cooking time left.

Cheese, nut, and fruit plates, such as Stilton with pears and walnuts, Gorgonzola with fresh figs and hazelnuts, or mascarpone with cherries and almonds.

Sorbets or granitas (see recipe, p. 106) garnished with nicely cut fresh fruit: try lemon sorbet with watermelon balls, mango sorbet with fresh raspberries, or coconut sorbet with diced pineapple.

Ice cream garnished with toasted nuts or coconut, shaved chocolate, sliced ripe fruit such as peaches, plums, nectarines, apricots, cherries, or bananas. Delicious vanilla whipped cream in a shake-and-spray can from France is now available in many cheese shops and specialty food stores.

Silpat and parchment keep sweet and savory baked foods from sticking to the pan and make for easy cleanup and multiple use of the same pan.

A heat-proof "spoonula" does the work of two utensils: you can stir a sauce or stew in the pan while it's cooking, then use it to scrape the food out and onto a platter or bowl.

The microplane grater is handy for cheese, ginger, garlic, and citrus zest.

All are widely available.

Coordinating Table Settings

A few years ago at Dragon Rock, I came across my father's original, unpublished table-setting thesis in that vast cavern known as our basement. Written in the 1950s, I believe many of his remarks to be relevant today, and I have edited for you the ideas I believe to be both interesting and of concern for those who keep house today.

On an average of three times a day, millions of tables are arranged for dining. The repetition of this task has stirred in all of us a desire for variation. Manufacturers continue to supply an endless variety of merchandise to tempt the bored consumer. Publications and merchandisers are also providing many ideas and products that are beginning to build table setting into a popular indoor activity.

All of this energy is producing more artistic and quite clever table settings, some of which are becoming so bizarre that it is often difficult to eat at them as well as on them. In response to this, I feel it is appropriate to review my father's original thesis. When he wrote it, he thought it advisable to attempt to analyze what a table setting should be, creating what he thought to be a "reasonable" basic plan susceptible to sufficient variation.

Aside from placing food on the table for orderly serving and eating, there are two basic purposes of table service:

1. **Forming the background for the food to show it off in the best way.**

2. **Establishing a mood for the meal, or for the food or for both.**

Many settings are possible that attempt both of the above, but it seemed to Russel that in practice, number 1 is very limited. Food may be set off to its truest values by definite means that permit some variation, but not an enormous amount. Number 2 offers an endless variety, but such settings must establish limitations or they easily detract from the food and spoil the whole meal.

In setting forth the limits for table service, it is best to show off all of the foods at their true values. All colors are present, with earth colors predominating in cooked foods. For the most part, textures are wet and glistening, but all are there.

The shapes of foods served in their natural form are all amorphous, irregular, and nongeometric. This is the commodity we must set off. In design, the problem is mainly one of contrasting or complementing. The following are the various elements that comprise the setting.

COMPOSITION: SHAPE, COLOR, TEXTURE

Dinnerware

Designed in practical terms of handling and washing, the shapes of dishes should be regular and geometric, not amorphous. And they should be shapes that will best hold each food. They should be unobtrusive—not so hard in line or shape as to attract more attention than the food. They should never be disturbing; because food is so active and alive in form and line, they should be quiet.

Shapes should be those that will keep food warm as well as those that present the food at its best. They should be soft, not sharp turns of surface that cast strong shadow contrasts. Undecorated dishes with perfectly flat, untextured glazes will best show off food textures. Dishes should be large enough that a border of plain surface is left around the food to best display the shapes, sizes, etc.

In theory, the perfect color for dishes is a middle value of gray, although any shade from white through black will set off food colors better than a color. White makes the colors opaque; black gives food colors a transparent brilliance.

The texture that contrasts best with most foods is a matte or dull finish, such as a matte or semi-matte glaze. Another possible texture and color combination is a gray metal such as aluminum: butler-brushed and anodized; very dull pewter; or dull silver-glazed pottery.

Metals should be dull, or reflections form a pattern that detracts from the food. Some dry-textured foods, including bread, are best displayed on a glossy surface such as glass. However, glass should be processed to reduce reflection.

To visually set off food to its truest value, several materials can be equally effective, such as pottery, glass, plastics, paper, or metal. But other factors enter the picture, such as heat retention, durability of surface, etc.

At the present time, pottery remains the most satisfactory material for all-around use.

Glass conducts heat away from the food too fast for use in deeper containers such as cups, soup bowls, and hot food servers.

Plastics have too porous and soft a surface to withstand continual food staining and cutting.

Paper lacks durability and offers a poor surface even when finished with the best plastic resins.

Metal conducts heat so quickly that it is practical only for room-temperature dishes; even then, it scratches too easily to be useful for long.

Here are recommendations for the various items:

Soup Bowl: pottery, or plastic for a shorter life.

Dinner plate: pottery or glass.

Salad plate: pottery or glass, or plastic for a shorter life.

Cup: pottery or plastic for a shorter life.

Dessert bowl: pottery, glass, metal, or plastic.

Platters: pottery or glass.

Coffeepots or teapots: pottery, or plastic for a shorter life.

Beverage Containers

Visually, beverage containers for wine, water, milk, coffee, and tea should be transparent and finished with process that reduces reflection, to best show off the beverage's color. They should be low and wide—tumblers, not stemware. (Who can feel relaxed holding a stem glass?) If lower heat-conducting containers are desired, they should be of a matte-textured gray color for coffee or milk, white for coffee or tea, and black for milk or coffee with milk.

Table Surface

To leave all of the color interest to the food, the table surface should be of a gray, black, or white color similar to the dishes. The table's texture might be dull or semigloss, preferably shinier than the dishes. It may be cloth or soft paper, or a veneered or painted table surface. A cover might be black or a darker gray to set off and frame the gray plates. Never use place mats; they provide too many shapes on the table, and detract from the food. There should be plenty of open table space; the more there is, the greater importance the food takes on visually.

If a contrast is used in table surface and dishes, the flatware should be the same color as the table top, or transparent, in order to leave the dark background of the table to set off only the shape of the food containers, never to show off other disturbing shapes.

Flatware and Cutlery

Flatware and cutlery should be transparent if the material is sufficiently strong and durable, or a very dull-finished gray metal (such as anodized butler-finished aluminum), or butler-finished silver or stainless steel. If a black table surface is used, flatware might be a black-finished metal. Preferably, only the flatware needed for each course should be placed on the table at each serving. The flatware should be smooth-surfaced, plain with no decoration, comfortable, and curved in shape.

Napkins

In color, napkins should be the same as the cloth, table surface, or plates (middle gray, dark gray, black, or white) to extend the table color over the clothing of the diner. Texture should be as near as possible to that of the table surface yet soft for usability, such as cloth or very soft paper. They also should be large.

Centerpiece

The main object of interest on the table should be the food set before the diner. A centerpiece placed in the middle of the table, especially one with floral scents, becomes a distraction and diminishes the appeal of the food. However, if an arrangement is desired, place it at the end of the table in an inconspicuous container—a transparent glass or a bowl of the same color as the dishes or tabletop. If dessert consists of fruit in some form, an arrangement of fruit will remind the diners to "save room."

Lighting

Lighting should be directly above the center of the table to eliminate shadows on the food, and should be a color that will best show off the natural food colors.

Seating

Chairs should be comfortable but erect, like office posture chairs. They should be at least one foot apart, be well padded, and have arms so that the diner will not lean on the table and spoil the presentation of the food. The color of the chairs is not important unless parts of them show after the diner is seated (such as the arms), or unless there is an empty chair. In such cases, the best color would be that of the walls or tabletop.

Floor

The floor is so far away from the table that it does not compete much visually with the food. However, a bold pattern (as in tiles) or a bright color should never be present. Any dark color—including brown, black, or gray—is desirable, and the soft resilient texture of carpets or rubber is more relaxing. A foot rail under the table is comfortable.

Walls

The walls are more important than the floor because they come within the same line of vision as the food. They should be gray—or a neutral, natural brown texture such as wood, with not too bold a figure—or a very dark color, preferably warm in tone.

Such a setting looks extremely dull until the food is served, when the food is revealed in its truest values of color, texture, shape, and amount. This setting can be austere, severe, dignified—truly elegant. It is a table for the "simon-pure" epicure. But many diners are shocked at its starkness, which is not conducive to gaiety, warmth, or intimacy. When diners are taken from the informality of the cocktail setting to the severity of this table setting, some seem nonplussed and a little disturbed.

More friendliness may be given to this setting by such changes as those listed below—but not, however, without detracting from the food.

1. A table decoration placed at the end of the table, such as greens, will relieve some of the severity. White flowers or other forms of decoration are elegant without offering a great deal of color competition to the food.

2. Highly polished silver and shiny clear glass will lend a little sparkle along with glossy-textured glazes for the dishes.

3. Textured linens make the setting look friendlier.

4. Interest and style are achieved by alternating the courses on pottery, metal, glass, and plastic, or on white and black dishes. However, the sharp contrast of the latter detracts a lot from the interest of the food.

5. Candlelight may be used, giving a warmer atmosphere to the whole setting.

A table setting can, however, do more for food than set it off visually. Diverging somewhat from a strict setting of the food as described above, the choices of containers, and the table arrangement can relax the diner, thus making the food taste even better. By dramatizing the food and providing visual stimulation, the appetite can also be stimulated.

RELAXATION

An important factor in relaxation is color. Don't use full-intensity color. Even clear pastel shades are not relaxing. Grays are the only really relaxing colors. With gray colors, however, a complementary scheme of orange and blue is not as relaxing as an analogous one of orange and yellow.

Analogous schemes include purple and red, red and orange, orange and yellow, yellow and green, green and blue, and blue and purple. Of those schemes, the last two would be the least stimulating.

Self-colored schemes are even more restful; for instance, all different shades of yellow. This, however, can become heavy or too strong. If used to create a restful effect, subdue the colors, or use small amounts of color (i.e., a sheer, translucent green tablecloth instead of an opaque one). Using continuing textures lessens the dullness and hardness of a single color.

Even quieter color schemes are found in red and red-orange, red-orange and orange, orange and orange-yellow, orange-yellow and yellow, yellow and yellow-green, yellow-green and green, green and green-blue, green-blue and blue, blue and blue-violet, blue-violet and violet, violet and violet-red, violet-red and red.

Grays and blacks and white make a very quiet scheme, but some people find them too dignified for relaxation. This type of setting is one of analogous color and is restful if close values are used. A wider preparation of values can be more stimulating to the eye and may be used in such a way that they become quite disturbing.

Even quieter is an all-brown scheme, since it seems to offer less contrast to the colors of food than does gray. Many food colors contain brown; all colors are contained in brown. One type of brown scheme is a setting employing all neutral materials, such as natural woods, natural cloth—shantung, for instance—straw, terra-cotta, pottery, etc. This scheme can become disturbing or annoying, however, if an abundance of exaggerated texture is used. If relaxation is wanted, the texture should be chosen and combined carefully, using quiet textures or relieving those that are exaggerated with simple ones. Multicolored schemes should not be used if restfulness and relaxation are desired.

The arrangement of the table itself can contribute to relaxation and restfulness. Do not use place mats. They break up the table in line and form more than is necessary. Use a cloth, or leave the table bare; however, the softness of a cloth is more relaxing than a bare tabletop. The cloth should be unpatterned, either sheer or heavy.

When planning a new course, it is important to clear the table of all evidence of the former course, and it is best to keep serving containers at the end of the table rather than in the center. The set table should be quieter in pattern than a buffet table setting can be.

Look at the various other elements of the setting and see

what they can contribute to relaxation. In form, the dishes and food containers should be sturdy, squat, and thick. In line, the dishes should be low, not vertical, and should tend toward smooth curved surfaces rather than angular existing ones. They should not have a pattern or decoration, but rather a quietly textured or a plain glaze. Handles should be quietly shaped and easy to hold. A matching set, if quiet and well designed, is less disturbing than odd pieces.

STIMULATION

Concerning stimulating the appetite with color, psychologists maintain that some colors, especially red, are the best. I do not know the theory or basis for this. If red stimulates the emotions, it might also be true that native dynamic line and form should also have the same effect. I do not know how the effect of line, form, and color on appetite can be proven. However, if this theory were accepted, it would follow that, in order to stimulate the appetite, measures should be practiced that are opposite to those suggested above for relaxation.

Setting off the food and relaxation are two objectives that can be achieved together, although both place some limitations on each other. Visual stimulation is in direct opposition to relaxation and can also hinder the setting off of the food. Therefore, visual stimulation should be used with extreme care. Take caution to avoid placing striking and disturbing elements directly in front of the diner while he or she is eating.

Various means of visual stimulation that can be used in serving include the following:

1. Sudden changes in color or change of light- and dark-value texture and design, or material in the table service (plates, cups, glasses, and flatware).

2. Using different, unmatched designs in the serving pieces and serving implements. The design and size of these may even be exaggerated and highly decorative.

3. A visually stimulating arrangement of flowers or objects placed at the end of the table.

4. Use of orange in lights.

5. Implementing a general color scheme that is striking rather than soft-toned or analogous. This must be carefully planned to avoid diverting too much interest or color away from the food.

6. Striking accents in line, form, or color on some or all of the service in such a way as not to be visually disturbing when the food is eaten.

7. Placement or stimulating arrangements of the food in the serving containers and on the individual service.

Presentation of foods is the basic idea of any table setting. Anything, including pulling chairs up to the kitchen stove and diving into the pots with your bare hands, is a dramatization of serving. The simplest, most unstudied kind of setting provides an order for the serving and creates a sort of ritual. An elaborate, studied setting is justified, stimulating interest in the food and setting it off to advantage. If properly done, dramatization can make food taste better.

It seems that the rules of any kind of dramatization apply to table settings as well. On the table as on the stage, the proper details must be considered for each meal and each food. Don't use gold service and crystal for a simple meal cooked by Mama. The Broadway production of *The Miracle* did just that. Hundreds of actors and thousands of dollars were used to overdramatize a twelfth-century peasant miracle play. Too elaborate a table setting kills the delicate flavor of the meal.

While I have given many suggestions, keep in mind that it is nearly impossible to establish rules or offer concrete plans for an entire setting, à la Emily Post. It is too personal and intimate an art for this. You must know the menu, the cook, the guests, the dining room, the house, and the occasion. Sometimes, knowing all this, you can plan the setting and the service in advance. More often, I wait until just before the meal and proceed in a more or less impromptu manner. I have sometimes decided upon the service as each course came along. However, perhaps some broad principles can be established for the setting of tables that will dramatize the food and not diminish it.

Any attempt at a stimulating visual effect should directly set off the food; it should not be a general overall effect. Contrasting effects should not be too great or too many. For instance, if more than one color is used, introduce the second color with the serving of a particular course. Avoid setting before the individual diner any object that will command more visual attention than the food because of contrast in line, form, or color.

As a basis for table setting, one should have a complete set of dinnerware. It should be of one solid color with no pattern, not a harlequin or two-color combination. Possible accessory pieces and duplicates, such as saucers, bread and butters, and desserts can be in another color for occasional use. The best colors are white, gray, black, or brown, either in solid flat glazes or in textures. The shapes should be simple, neither period nor obtrusive, self-conscious modern.

The simplest method for dramatizing food is the serving dish. Various good ones should be collected. Of course, they must be selected with some consideration of the general set in mind, which is all the more reason for having a very simple set. These pieces need not match the set but may contrast with it. Select them to represent the particular character of food to be served and, of course, consider how well they set off the food in stage, color, etc.

In general, keep away from poorly designed modern servers such as red lobster dishes. It is mainly a matter of imagination and taste. A hit may be made with a black frying pan and an aluminum cover, or with a galvanized bucket full of foaming beer. Sometimes a food item is emphasized if special individual dishes are used for courses instead of a regular dinnerware set. For instance, modern plates for the salad, glass ice cream dishes, wooden bowls for berries, etc.

MOOD

In addition to setting off and dramatizing the food and relaxing and stimulating the diner, the table setting is often expected to express certain moods. It is possible for the table setting to do so effectively, providing not too many different moods are desired, and providing such devices are used to dramatize the food and are arranged so as not to detract too much from the food or from the relaxation of the diners. With proper consideration, the effects used to establish the desired moods may often be blended with those needed for setting off and dramatizing the food.

I believe that my father's study of the dining experience is as valid today as when he wrote it forty years ago.

With that said, one needs to understand that this thesis is merely a guideline, and that each diner, chef, and host must feel free to exhibit his or her own creativity whenever and wherever he or she sees fit. Right and wrong do not exist here, so, diner beware!

Over the years, food enthusiasts have become more sophisticated and have become interested in exploring a variety of venues to express individuality in both presentation and cooking. I believe all of this is acceptable and know that Russel would have felt the same way because—above all— he always endorsed creativity and experimentation.

In reality, our table was never set exactly as it was the time before, because we were always "improving" upon the visuals and the eating experience in general. I encourage you to do the same.

Index